LEGENDS OF WARFARE

AVIATION

P-39 Airacobra

Bell Fighter in WWII

DAVID DOYLE

SCHIFFER MILITARY

4880 Lower Valley Road ■ Atglen, PA 19310

Cover design by Justin Watkinson
Type set in Impact/Minion Pro/Univers LT Std
Front cover photo by Rich Kolasa

ISBN: 978-0-7643-6703-8
Printed in India

Published by Schiffer Publishing, Ltd.
4880 Lower Valley Road
Atglen, PA 19310
Phone: (610) 593-1777; Fax: (610) 593-2002
Email: Info@schifferbooks.com
Web: www.schifferbooks.com

For our complete selection of fine books on this and related subjects, please visit our website at www.schifferbooks.com. You may also write for a free catalog.

Schiffer Publishing's titles are available at special discounts for bulk purchases for sales promotions or premiums. Special editions, including personalized covers, corporate imprints, and excerpts, can be created in large quantities for special needs. For more information, contact the publisher.

We are always looking for people to write books on new and related subjects. If you have an idea for a book, please contact us at proposals@schifferbooks.com.

Acknowledgments

This book would not have been possible without the generous assistance of Stan Piet, Tom Kailbourn, Rich Kolasa, Scott Taylor, the staff at the National Archives and Records Administration, the American Aviation Historical Society, and Brett Stolle and the staff at the National Museum of the United States Air Force. In particular, I want to thank my wife, Denise, for the countless hours of scanning and support during this project.

Contents

Introduction

While the Bell P-39 remains a famed World War II aircraft, its legacy is often wrapped in myth and misinformation. Many think that the Soviets used the aircraft with great success as a tank buster—in reality, the Soviets *did* use the aircraft with great success, but most often in air-to-air combat against German aircraft. So great was the Soviet success with the P-39, some forget that the aircraft also served well for the British, Free French, and the United States, on whom this volume will focus.

Similarly, many enthusiasts point to the removal of the turbosupercharger from the aircraft as evidence of a conspiracy, either inside the Army Air Corps or by others in the aviation industry, to deny the Bell its rightful place in America's arsenal. In fact, Larry Bell himself thought this was the right decision, writing to George Lewis at NACA (predecessor of NASA) on January 17, 1940, that "from all indications the XP-39 will do over 400 miles per hour (even) with 1,150 horsepower. All of the changes were improvements[,] and we have eliminated a million and one problems by removal of the turbosupercharger."

The P-39 was created in response to the US Army Air Corps Circular Proposal X-609, issued in February 1937. This circular was crafted by Lt. Benjamin S. Kelsey, fighter project officer in the Engineering Section, Material Command, Wright Field, and Captain Gordon P. Saville, fighter tactics instructor for the Air Corps Tactical School. The two men employed for the first time "interceptor" in their specifications, thereby bypassing an Air Corps mandatory (and arbitrary) limit of 500 pounds as a maximum weight for all guns and ammunition. The specification outlined in Proposal X-609 called for a level airspeed of 360 mph at altitude, the ability to climb to 20,000 feet in six minutes, tricycle landing gear, a minimum 1,000 pounds of armament, including a cannon, and the use of an Allison V-1710 liquid-cooled engine equipped with a turbosupercharger. Perhaps because of Kelsey's position, despite using the new appellation "interceptor," the proposal number (609) was, like all 600-series proposals, a "pursuit" proposal, and of course the resultant aircraft carried a P for pursuit designation (the F for fighter designation did not come into being until 1948).

Contemporaneous with the XP-39 was the XP-38, which was created in response to Air Corps Specification X-608 (the XP-39 was created to specification X-609). Clarence "Kelly" L. Johnson and his design team at Lockheed began development of the XP-38 in January 1937, and the US Army Air Corps issued a contract to Lockheed on June 23 of that year to build one prototype. The XP-38 was powered by twin turbosupercharged Allison engines. *National Museum of the United States Air Force*

The Curtiss XP-40 was another of the generation's Allison-powered pursuit aircraft. Created by heavily modifying the tenth production P-36 Curtiss Hawk, the XP-40 first flew on October 15, 1938. *National Museum of the United States Air Force*

Bell Aircraft, then in its second year, was one of three firms to respond to Circular X-609, competing against Curtiss and Seversky. Seversky offered five designs in response to the circular, while Curtiss and Bell each offered two designs. A three-officer panel consisting of Lt. Col. Adlai Gilkeson, Lt. Col. Gerald Brower, and Captain Saville evaluated the various proposals presented. The panel determined that the two Bell proposals offered the greatest promise.

Bell's responses were their Model 3 and Model 4. The sleek Model 3 looked more like a racing aircraft of the era than it did a combat aircraft. The low-profile canopy was set well back along the fuselage, aft of the wing. In this design, the Allison engine was mounted over the wing, and thus ahead of the cockpit. A 5½-foot extension shaft connected the engine to the propeller while allowing room for the proposed 25 mm cannon armament, which was to fire through the propeller hub. A review of the Model 3 mockup on May 24, 1937, showed that the layout severely limited the pilot's visibility.

Bell's other entry, the Model 4, also had a midengine, but the cockpit was moved to a position forward of the engine. Shifting the engine rearward required the use of a 10-foot-long extension shaft but also permitted the armament bay to be enlarged. The driving force behind this design, noted for its clean, streamlined nose configuration, was Bell chief designer Robert J. Woods and his assistant, Harland M. Poyer. Woods and Poyer had observed a demonstration of American Armament Corporation's 37 mm cannon at Aberdeen Proving Ground, Maryland, in 1935. Although American Armament's weapon was a variation of the World War I Puteaux cannon, the Bell men were impressed by the potential of a 37 mm autocannon. The John Browning–designed, Colt-produced T9 37 mm autocannon was chosen for use in the new aircraft, as well as the Bell YFM-1 Airacuda.

In order to keep frontal area of the aircraft at a minimum, the Model 4 cockpit was narrower than recommended by the Army Handbook, requiring approval of the deviation. The cockpit design was also unique in that it featured two automobile-type doors for access. Like the Model 3, the Model 4 design stipulated tricycle landing gear.

The US Army Air Corps issued contract AC-10341 for a single example of the Model 4, designated XP-39, on October 7, 1937, assigning it serial number 38-326. The XP-39 was fabricated at Bell's plant on Elmwood Avenue in Buffalo, New York, under the supervision of project engineer Frank M. "Sal" Salisbury, and was ready for ground testing in late 1938. Engine tests in the aircraft were begun on December 4, and as a result of those tests some changes were made to the extension shaft installation and engine cowl. At the conclusion of the engine tests, the aircraft was dismantled, crated, and shipped by rail to Wright Field, Dayton, Ohio, arriving there on December 27, 1938.

The Air Corps carefully inspected the prototype and, as a result, insisted on adding reinforcing strips to the canopy. When engine testing began at Wright Field on February 8, the Allison continued to be problematic and thus was returned to Allison for modification, with the company not returning the engine to Wright Field until April 1939. This considerably delayed the program. The XP-39's maiden flight finally occurred on April 6, 1939, with retired Navy pilot James Taylor at the controls. That flight, and one the following day before Gen. Henry "Hap" Arnold, showed that the engine oil cooler installation was inadequate and would need redesign.

Although the aircraft fell short of its top-speed goal, achieving about 375 mph, the design showed promise. Keeping with the previous aircraft-naming theme, Bell dubbed the aircraft the Airacobra.

The XP-39 was the prototype of the P-39, and the Bell Aircraft Company produced one example at its plant in Wheatfield, New York, near Niagara Falls. This aircraft bore a strong resemblance to early-production P-39s, with some exceptions, including the taller canopy; the lack of an air scoop on top of the fuselage, aft of the canopy; the propeller spinner, which came to a point, with no cutout for a nose weapon; and the cuffed propeller blades. Other noticeable differences between the prototype and production P-39s were the smaller vertical tail on the prototype and the prominent intake scoop on the left side of the fuselage, aft of the cockpit, for the turbosupercharger mated to the Allison V-1710-17 in-line engine. *American Aviation Historical Society*

The turbosupercharger scoop on the XP-39 is viewed from another angle. A shroud covered the engine exhausts. No armament was installed. Cutouts on the nose landing-gear doors provided clearance for the nosewheel when retracted. *American Aviation Historical Society*

The XP-39 displays its stance on the tricycle landing gear. Attached to the propeller spinner were three streamlined fairings that matched the profile of the propeller cuffs and eliminated the traditional gap between the spinner and propeller blades. *National Museum of the United States Air Force*

The XP-39 had an odd, split-type main landing-gear door. On the right side of the fuselage was an air intake for the radiator and oil cooler; this intake was different in shape from the turbosupercharger air scoop, seen here on the left side. *National Museum of the United States Air Force*

PROOF PRINT

In an effort to improve the performance of the aircraft, the XP-39 was placed inside the NACA wind tunnel at the Langley Memorial Aeronautics Laboratory, Langley Field, Virginia, for testing. The man at the bottom of this August 9, 1939, image gives a sense of scale to the aircraft and the fixture that held it in place in the wind tunnel. *NASA*

NACA
18423

PROOF PRINT

Prior to the wind tunnel tests, the propeller and all protrusions were removed from the fuselage of the XP-39. These tests led to development of the XP-39B. *NASA*

CHAPTER 2
XP-39B

The XP-39 fell short of the 400 mph top speed Bell was aiming for, reaching only 375 mph without armament and with only a partial fuel load. In June 1939, Gen. Henry "Hap" Arnold ordered that the XP-39 be tested in NACA wind tunnels, with an eye toward increasing speed by reducing parasitic drag. NACA made several recommendations toward reducing drag, including reducing wingspan, lengthening the fuselage, and lowering the cockpit. The most notable change, however, concerned the turbosupercharger cooling duct bulging from the left side of the fuselage. Regarding the duct, NACA wrote, "It is imperative to enclose the supercharger within the airplane with an efficient duct system for cooling the rotor and discharging the cooling air and exhaust gases." The problem was, there was no space within the airframe for the turbosupercharger. The XP-39 was extensively rebuilt following the NACA recommendations,

becoming the XP-39B. The General Electric B-5 two-stage turbosupercharger used on the XP-39 gave way to a single-stage gear-driven supercharger. Whereas a turbosupercharger is driven by engine exhaust, with a minimal "cost" in base horsepower, superchargers being mechanically driven do consume some of the engine's output horsepower, although the power gained from supercharging outweighs the power consumed. The engine of the XP-39 was the Allison V-1710-17 (E2), while the XP-39B flew with the V-1710-37 (E5). The new power plant performed well at low and medium altitudes but fell off rapidly as altitudes increased, primarily due to its single-stage supercharging. At the time of the XP-39B's first flight on November 25, 1939, US air doctrine was based on the assumption that the vast oceans would protect the United States from bomber attack, and the XP-39B would still be adept at supporting ground troops.

Following wind tunnel tests of the XP-39 at Langley Field, Virginia, in 1939, Bell revised the airframe of that prototype aircraft, redesignating it the XP-39B. The XP-39B featured a redesigned canopy with a reinforced frame and a lower and longer profile; a wingspan reduced by 1 foot, 10 inches; and a fuselage that was lengthened by 1 foot, 1 inch.

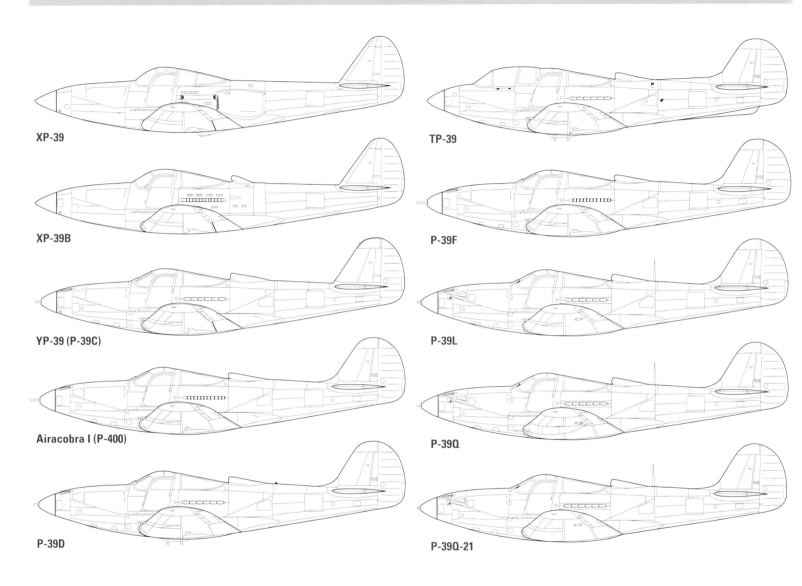

XP-39

XP-39B

YP-39 (P-39C)

Airacobra I (P-400)

P-39D

TP-39

P-39F

P-39L

P-39Q

P-39Q-21

In addition to the length being changed, the turbosupercharger was eliminated from the XP-39B, and the radiator and oil-cooler air scoop on the right side of the fuselage were replaced by new air scoops in the wing roots. Other changes included a new engine, the V-1710-39, and new main and nose landing-gear doors. *National Museum of the United States Air Force*

Initially, the XP-39B had a single door on front of the front landing-gear strut, with two small doors at the rear of the landing-gear well. With the elimination of the turbosupercharger and its air scoop, a carburetor air scoop was added to the top of the fuselage. *National Museum of the United States Air Force*

The XP-39B featured a lower-profile canopy and, behind it, an air intake scoop for the downdraft carburetor. Eventually, a new nose landing-gear door arrangement was installed on the XP-39B, with two large doors along the landing-gear well and a small door at the top front of the landing-gear strut. Numerous air louvers were above and below the right exhaust. *National Museum of the United States Air Force*

The XP-39B was destroyed as the result of a hard landing on August 6, 1940, with Captain Ernest Warburton, chief of the Wright Field test unit, at the controls. By then, however, additional aircraft were already on order, the US Army Air Corps having ordered thirteen service test aircraft on April 27, 1939. Twelve of these aircraft were to have been powered by the Allison V-1710-17 turbosupercharged engine as used in the XP-39B. These aircraft, Bell Model 12, would be designated YP-39 by the military. As built, they were patterned after the XP-39B. Externally, the most noticeable change was a wider chord on the vertical tail.

As initially ordered, one of the thirteen was to have been a YP-39A, featuring a 1,150 hp Allison V-1710-31 with a gear-driven supercharger, but no turbosupercharger. The higher-than-usual step of ratio of the -31 engine's supercharger was supposed to make the engine suitable for use at high altitudes. This made the engine comparable to the V-1710-33 engine used in the Curtiss P-40, P-40B, and P-40C. It was known that high-altitude performance would suffer some as a result, but this was permissible by the new standards, Specification C-616, under which the aircraft were procured.

Ultimately, the plan to install the V-1710-33 engine in the YP-39 was abandoned, and all thirteen utilized the 1,090 hp Allison V-1710-37 (E5) engine and Curtiss Electric propeller.

The first YP-39, serial number 40-027, lifted into the air on September 13, 1940, a week after its completion. It would be lost in a crash just over a month later, on October 18, when the Bell test pilot was forced to bail out due to malfunctioning landing gear.

The last YP-39 was delivered on December 16, 1940, and all the YP-39s were used in an evaluation and testing role, with none of them being assigned to Army service squadrons.

Some of the YP-39 aircraft actually had armament installed, unlike the previous experimental aircraft, which had been completed and flown without weaponry. The armament, all of which was mounted in the nose, included a pair of .30-caliber machine guns, a pair of .50-caliber machine guns, and a 37 mm cannon. That cannon, the T9 built by Colt, had been standardized on December 28, 1940, as the "Gun, Automatic, 37 mm, M4."

Bell delivered the thirteen YP-39s, serial numbers 40-027 to 40-039, from September to December 1940, including this example sporting red and white stripes and a blue vertical bar on the rudder, as well as a large landing-gear door on the nose strut. Like the XP-39B, the YP-39s lacked a turbosupercharger, in keeping with the US Army Air Corps' prewar emphasis on ground-attack aircraft instead of fighter aircraft, for which supercharged engines were essential for attaining satisfactory performance at high altitudes. The YP-39 in this photo is an early example without armament. Subsequently, YP-39s were fitted with five guns in the nose: a 37 mm cannon, two .50-caliber machine guns, and two .30-caliber machine guns. *Stan Piet collection*

A Bell YP-39 was photographed on October 16, 1940. The nose landing-gear doors on this example comprised two large doors mounted on the fuselage and a small door near the top front of the landing-gear strut. The nose was smooth and devoid of air vents. *American Aviation Historical Society*

The same YP-39 in the preceding photo is viewed from the left rear. The main landing-gear doors comprised two pieces: a large door on each main landing-gear strut, and a small door on the inboard edge of each main landing-gear bay. *American Aviation Historical Society*

A test pilot in the cockpit of a Bell YP-39 peers down at the cameraman. "US Army" was painted under the wings. The inboard air intake in each wing root led to the Prestone radiator, while the outboard intake in each wing root supplied air to an oil cooler. *American Aviation Historical Society*

One of the thirteen YP-39 service-test prototype aircraft produced by Bell skims above the clouds. These aircraft were built to XP-39B standards but with an enlarged vertical tail and the replacement of the Allison V-1710-39 engine with the V-1710-37 (E5). *National Museum of the United States Air Force*

Seen from above while in flight, this YP-39 features the prewar red, white, and blue stripes on the rudder and the red circle within the white star on the national insignia. The skin of the aircraft was natural-aluminum finish, but the control surfaces—the ailerons, elevators, and rudder—were covered with fabric doped with an aluminum-colored paint. The ailerons, in particular, show up in this photo as a different tone than the aluminum skin. A close examination of the photograph reveals that a wire antenna is present from the top of the frame at the center of the canopy to the leading edge of the vertical stabilizer. *American Aviation Historical Society*

Armament was added to YP-39s during their testing, and this one has what appear to be a 37 mm cannon and machine guns in the nose and panels on the leading edges of the wings, indicating the possible presence, or intention to install, machine guns in the wings. *National Museum of the United States Air Force*

A YP-39 presents a very sleek, streamlined appearance in flight, due in part to its highly polished propeller spinner. The propellers on YP-39s were the Curtiss Electric. This is likely one of the early examples of this model, since it lacks armament. *American Aviation Historical Society*

Flying over an airfield, this YP-39 has its landing gear and flaps extended. These were split flaps: essentially, hinged panels on the bottom surface of the wings only; the tops of the wings are not cut out to accommodate split flaps. *American Aviation Historical Society*

At Bell Aircraft, a YP-39 is in the foreground. A close view is provided of its rudder, vertical stabilizer, and elevators, as well as the highly polished carburetor air intake. To the right is the XFL-1 Airabonita, and in the background is a Bell YFM-1A interceptor. *American Aviation Historical Society*

A factory photograph intended to show the installation of the oil temperature regulator also reveals a good deal of information on the structure of the middle part of the Airacobra's fuselage. At the bottom is the wing's center section, which housed the oil coolers. *American Aviation Historical Society*

The lower part of the instrument panel is displayed in an October 1940 view. To the left of the instrument panel is the ignition switch, while immediately to the right of the instrument panel are the airspeed tube selector switch and vacuum pump selector switch. Below these features in the background are the rudder pedals. To the top left are switches for various systems. In the foreground is the control column, a yoke that at its bottom, hidden from view by the boot, straddled the driveshaft running from the engine forward to the gearbox. *American Aviation Historical Society*

An October 1940 photograph shows the instrument panel of an early Airacobra. The layout of the panel would remain largely unchanged through subsequent models of the P-39. In the large gaps to the sides of the central panel are machine-gun charging handles. *American Aviation Historical Society*

This Airacobra appears to have been a YP-39, since its nomenclature stencil has a two-letter prefix in its model name: most likely YP. On the pilot's door is the insignia of the Air Corps Technical School. A faded aircraft number, 174, is present on the nose and on the vertical stabilizer. *National Museum of the United States Air Force*

The same YP-39 of the Air Corps Technical School shown in the preceding photo flies near Denver, Colorado. The code 42ED on the vertical tail stood for the 42nd School Squadron, a training unit. The machine guns in the nose were removed, and fairings were fitted over their openings. However, the muzzle of the 37 mm cannon is present. *National Archives*

This Bell YP-39, serial number 40-032, bears the insignia of the Air Corps Technical School on its fuselage. Fairings are fitted over the openings for the machine guns on top of the nose, and the 37 mm cannon has been removed. "Chanute Field" is stenciled above the nomenclature stencil. *American Aviation Historical Society*

Armorers service the guns of an early Airacobra with four machine guns in the nose: probably a YP-39, but perhaps a P-39C. The two .30-caliber machine guns are on the bench, while the .50-caliber guns are still in the nose. *Stan Piet collection*

CHAPTER 4
P-39C

On August 10, 1939, the Army Air Corps ordered eighty more of the aircraft, the first true production order. The first model produced under this order was the Bell Model 13, and the eighty Model 13s that were ordered were assigned Air Corps serial numbers 40-2971 through 40-3050. Initially, these aircraft were designated P-45. However, congressional policy at that time was that funding was available only for already-existing aircraft models, so wisely the decision was made to retain the P-39 designation, the new model being dubbed P-39C.

The new aircraft would be the first of the P-39 type to leave the factory wearing camouflage, with a Neutral Gray underside and Olive Drab upper surfaces.

The P-39C, which first flew in January 1941, was almost identical to the YP-39, except its power plant was the 1,150 hp Allison V-1710-35 (E4). Armament was the same as that on the YP-39, and like its predecessors it lacked armor and self-sealing fuel tanks. Those two omissions resulted in the aircraft being deemed not combat ready, and the eighty-plane contract was amended to include provision for both. The sixty aircraft remaining on the order would incorporate these and other improvements and were designated P-39D; they will be discussed later in this book. The bulk of the P-39Cs were assigned to the 40th Pursuit Squadron, 31st Pursuit Group, although the British did get three examples: 40-2981, 40-2983, and 40-2984. Ultimately, the P-39C aircraft were redesignated RP-39C—the "R" denoting restricted to noncombat use.

Workmen roll out a P-39C, one of only twenty aircraft produced of that model. The first production model of the Airacobra, the P-39C was built virtually to YP-39 standards and originally was designated the P-45. Most of the P-39Cs served as service-test aircraft with the 31st Pursuit Group, 40th Pursuit Squadron, at Selfridge Field, Michigan. The ports for the two .30-caliber machine guns and two .50-caliber machine guns are visible on the nose, and the 37 mm cannon muzzle protrudes through the propeller. On the tail are markings signifying the thirty-third aircraft of the 31st Pursuit Group. *American Aviation Historical Society*

This P-39C lacks visible markings other than the national insignia on the side of the fuselage. The paint scheme was Olive Drab on the upper surfaces and Neutral Gray on the lower surfaces. The propeller blades were left in natural metal. No guns are mounted. *National Museum of the United States Air Force*

The wings of the P-39C, like those of other Airacobras, had a dihedral of 4 degrees. The plane's nose-high attitude on the ground and the relatively low cockpit canopy limited somewhat the pilot's forward field of vision during taxiing and takeoff. *National Museum of the United States Air Force*

The P-39C in the two preceding photographs is viewed from the left side. The skin of the Airacobras had a smooth appearance. It was flush-riveted and consisted of 0.051-gauge formed aluminum in the nose and under the pilot's seat and 0.32 gauge elsewhere. *National Museum of the United States Air Force*

The exhausts on the P-39C were formed from six stubs on each side of the engine. The elevators and rudder were formed of extruded ribs fastened to a beam and covered with fabric. In addition, the rudder had formed aluminum upper and lower cap pieces. *National Museum of the United States Air Force*

The nosewheel on Airacobras was a castering, nonsteerable design. Operation of the nose and main landing gear was electrical. The retracting link of the nose gear is in view. The nose and main landing gear employed Cleveland Pneumatic Tool oil-air shock struts. *American Aviation Historical Society*

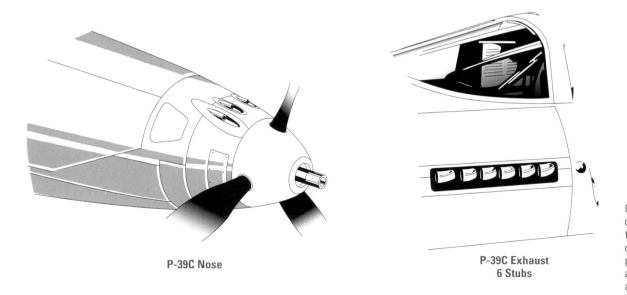

P-39C Nose

**P-39C Exhaust
6 Stubs**

Characteristics of the P-39C are depicted in these illustrations. To the left is the nose, with a 37 mm cannon firing through the propeller spinner, above which are two .50-caliber machine guns and two .30-caliber machine guns. To the right are the exhausts, with six stubs.

Slightly raised fairings over the machine gun openings on top of the nose of this P-39C are discernible. Numerous small, hinged, reinforced access doors were distributed on the undersides of the wings, which were clad with formed aluminum, 0.025 to 0.051 gauge. *American Aviation Historical Society*

Ground crewmen manhandle a P-39C of the 31st Pursuit Group onto a flight line with other P-39Cs at Selfridge Field, Michigan. A man to the front of the plane is manipulating a tow bar attached to the nose landing gear. All the Airacobras have the slightly raised fairings installed over the .30-caliber and .50-caliber machine gun openings on top of the nose, and all the aircraft lack the 37 mm cannon. Interestingly, the main landing-gear doors have been removed from the struts of the closest aircraft in line, revealing the spoked wheels. *National Archives*

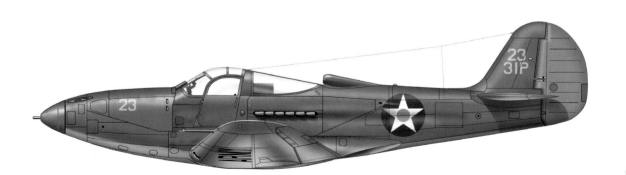

One of the twenty P-39Cs produced bears markings for the 31st Pursuit Group, based at Selfridge Field, Michigan. The plane was painted in a two-color camouflage of Olive Drab over Neutral Gray. "US" was painted under the right wing, and "ARMY," as seen here, was on the bottom of the left wing.

In a color companion photo to the preceding view, P-39Cs of the 31st Pursuit Group are parked on a tarmac at Selfridge Field, Michigan, sometime after January 1941, when this model of Airacobra made its first flight. Aircraft number 22 has joined the line next to number 23, which was the closest aircraft in the preceding photo. Number 22 has solid wheel covers on its main landing gear, hiding the spoked wheels. In late 1941, the yellow coloring scheme for aircraft and group numbers on this group's P-39Cs was revised to a less conspicuous scheme of flat black. *Stan Piet collection*

Two pilots compare notes on a winter day while a third pilot in the nearest Airacobra, an unarmed P-39C, warms up the plane's Allison engine. The next plane in line is a bare-aluminum YP-39 with the muzzle of a 37 mm cannon protruding through the spinner. *Stan Piet collection*

CHAPTER 5
Airacobra I / P-400

Larry Bell's fledgling firm was desperate for business, and European nations were hungry for aircraft in 1939. The Bell Model 14 was intended to address both of these issues. This export model of the Airacobra caught the attention of the French Armée de l'Air, which ordered 200 of the Model 14s on October 8, 1939—and according to some sources, the order was accompanied by a $2 million down payment.

On April 13, 1940, British Purchasing Commission representatives, impressed by the predicted performance outlined in Circular Proposal X-609, placed an order for 675 of the aircraft sight unseen.

France would fall before their Airacobras could be delivered, and the order was taken over by the British, who incorporated them into the 675 aircraft that the Commonwealth had on order.

The British aircraft, which carried the appellation Airacobra I, utilized a Hispano-Suiza 20 mm cannon rather than the US 37 mm weapon. The aircraft were powered by the Allison V-1710-E4 (-35). The first of the aircraft built to the foreign orders reached England in July 1941, just a few days after the three transferred P-39Cs had arrived. Testing began immediately, and just as immediately disappointment over the aircraft's performance set in. Even though the Airacobras were comparable to both the Spitfire VB and a captured Bf 109E during low-altitude trials, above 15,000 feet the performance of the Bell product fell off rapidly, and of course the aircraft was 33 mph slower than anticipated.

The Airacobras were assigned to No. 601 Squadron, County of London, who flew their first operational mission with them on October 9, 1941, shooting up an enemy trawler. The most significant issue with the Airacobras was a change in compass alignment due to the firing of the guns, although it was noted that there was a need for flash suppressors for the nose guns and flame dampers for the exhausts.

Ultimately, the British decided that they did not want the Airacobras, even before all the aircraft had left the United States. The British decided to transfer the bulk of the aircraft to the Soviet Union. The Soviets put the Airacobras to good use. In fact, the Russians would go on to order many more examples.

In the USSR, the Airacobra would enjoy considerable success, not as a "tank buster" as often assumed and erroneously reported, but rather as a fighter, facing—and besting—Luftwaffe aircraft that were attacking Soviet troops in ground attack and close-support missions. Not only were many Russian aces made in Airacobras, eight of them shot down thirty or more German aircraft each, with Soviet ace Grigory Andreyevich Rechkalov scoring forty-eight of his fifty-four confirmed victories in an Airacobra. Few people realize that of all the various types of fighter aircraft produced in the United States during World War II, the Airacobra would score the most victories, outpacing the F6F, Corsair, and Mustang. This vacuum of data is largely the result of the dearth of information flowing from Russia from wartime until the late twentieth century.

After the Japanese attack on Pearl Harbor, the US Army Air Corps was desperate for aircraft and took over 179 of the Airacobra Is ordered by the British, and not yet shipped to the Russians. The aircraft, retaining their British serial numbers and camouflage, were designated P-400 by the Americans. Many were used stateside for training, but some saw combat in the Pacific with the 8th Fighter Group in Australia and New Guinea, the 347th Fighter Group on Guadalcanal, and the 35th Fighter Group in New Guinea, and a further handful saw service in Europe.

An Airacobra I destined for the British is prepared for flight at Bell's Wheatfield, New York, plant by test pilot Robert M. "Bob" Stanley. This model of aircraft would prove a great disappointment to the British when they learned that it had been stripped of its supercharger. The nose armament specified by the British, a Hispano 20 mm gun and two .303-caliber machine guns, have not yet been installed, but the two .303-caliber machine guns in the right wing appear to be present. British camouflage paint and markings have already been applied, including the fin flashes and the roundels. The RAF serial number on the rear of the fuselage is hidden by the wing. This example has six exhaust stubs; most Airacobra IIs had twelve exhaust stubs per side. *Stan Piet collection*

This Airacobra was Bell Aircraft's airframe no. 14, employed as a prototype for the P-400. It carried civil registration number NX-BA14 on the tail. What appears to be a spent-casing ejector port and an unusual casing deflector are to the front of the door. *American Aviation Historical Society*

A pilot, probably Bob Stanley, hoists himself up on the wing of Airacobra I, serial number AH621, at Wheatfield, New York, in 1941. The painters at Bell Aircraft who applied the Dark Earth and Dark Green over Sky camouflage had extended the Sky too far upward. *American Aviation Historical Society*

Airacobra I, serial number AH577, of No. 601 Squadron RAF, rests on the field at RAF Duxford, Cambridgeshire, England, on August 21, 1941. On August 8, 1941, the squadron had taken delivery of this aircraft, which became the first Airacobra I to fly with the unit.

The RAF's No. 601 Squadron displays its new Bell Airacobra I aircraft for members of the press at RAF Duxford on October 17, 1941. The muzzles of the 20 mm cannons protrude from the spinners of the propellers. Aircraft letters are to the front of the side doors.

The serial number of this Airacobra I is partially obscured by the shadow cast by the horizontal stabilizer and elevator. The fillet at the bottom front edge of the vertical stabilizer was a new feature. *National Museum of the United States Air Force*

An Airacobra I in RAF camouflage rests on a tarmac. The serial number has not yet been applied on the rear of the fuselage. The weapons have not been installed, but the right blast tube for a .303-caliber machine gun is visible on top of the nose. *American Aviation Historical Society*

The Airacobra I with serial number DS173, one of three P-39Cs delivered to the British for firing trials with the 37 mm cannon, rests on the field at Colerne, Wiltshire, England, on July 13, 1941. After trials, this Airacobra I served with No. 601 Squadron RAF.

Airacobra I AH577, squadron/aircraft code UF-M, of No. 601 Squadron RAF, conducts a photo-op flight on August 21, 1941. This is one of a series of photographs of that squadron's Airacobra I aircraft taken by Mr. B. J. Daventry, an RAF photographer, on that date.

Airacobra I, serial number AH576, of No. 601 Squadron RAF, seen at RAF Duxford on August 21, 1941, was detached to Reid & Sigrist Ltd. for trials on September 7. This aircraft never saw further service, however, since it was written off on October 5, 1941.

Ground crewmen inspect an Airacobra I of No. 601 Squadron RAF at Duxford on August 21, 1941. In addition to the 20 mm cannon and two .303-caliber machine guns in the nose, the Airacobra I had two .303-caliber machine guns in each wing.

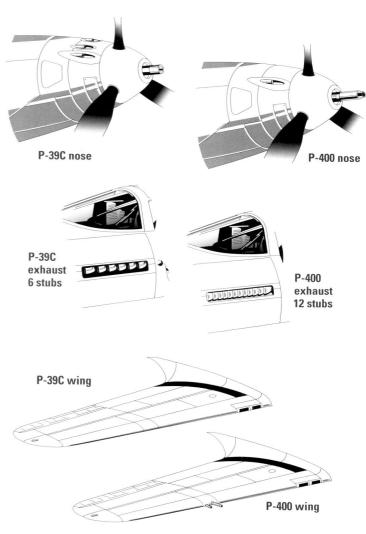

P-39C nose

P-400 nose

P-39C exhaust 6 stubs

P-400 exhaust 12 stubs

P-39C wing

P-400 wing

This Airacobra I, serial number AH621, performs a demonstration flight from the Bell Aircraft factory in Wheatfield, New York, in 1941. It is not clear how the staff at Bell decided on the unusually high, and incorrect, application of Sky paint to the fuselage. *Stan Piet collection*

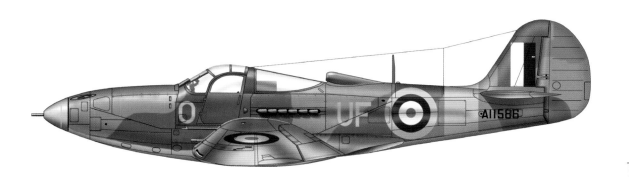

The Airacobra I with serial number AH586 and fuselage code UF-O served with No. 601 Squadron, based at RAF Duxford, in 1941.

Many of the 179 Airacobra I aircraft that the Royal Air Force declined to take delivery of but that the US Army Air Forces accepted as P-400s saw combat service, including these P-400s of the 67th Fighter Squadron, photographed on Guadalcanal in October 1942. *National Archives*

P-400s preparing for a mission to North Africa are being serviced at the 91st Bomb Group base at Bassingbourne, England, on March 10, 1943. The national insignia on the planes has the yellow borders associated with USAAF aircraft in North Africa. *National Archives*

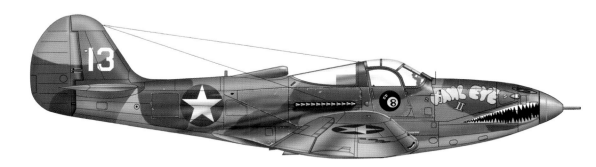

This Bell P-400 bore the nicknames "Pat" on the left side and "Wahl Eye II" on the right. A decoration with shark's mouth and eye has been painted on each side of the nose, and an eight ball is on each door. The pilot was Lt. Eugene Wahl, of the 39th Fighter Squadron, 35th Fighter Group, based at Twelve Mile Aerodrome in New Guinea.

CHAPTER 6
P-39D

By late 1940, World War II had been underway in Europe for almost two years, and combat experiences in the conflict were being studied by the US Army Air Corps. It was quickly revealed that the P-39C was not sufficiently armed or protected for combat use as a ground support aircraft. On September 13, 1940, 394 Bell Model 15 aircraft were ordered, which were designated P-39D. On the next day the earlier eighty-plane contract was modified, such that the final sixty aircraft on that order would be built as P-39Ds as well.

The P-39D differed from its predecessor in several details, including the addition of bulletproof windshields, armor protection for the pilot, the use of self-sealing fuel tanks (even though this change brought with it a 33 percent reduction in fuel capacity—which in turn brought about the addition of provisions to carry an external drop tank, or bomb), and a notable increase in armament.

The 37 mm cannon that fired through the hub of the propeller was retained, although the Curtiss Electric propeller itself grew to a 10-foot, 5-inch model. The twin nose-mounted .50-caliber machine guns were retained as well. The nose-mounted .30-caliber machine guns, however, were moved to the wings, where they were joined by a second pair of .30-caliber machine guns. Ammunition available for all guns was increased as well. The length of the fuselage was increased slightly to 30 feet, 2 inches, and a small dorsal fin was added just forward of the vertical stabilizer. All these changes pushed the Airacobra's weight up 245 pounds.

Two further batches of P-39Ds were built especially for Lend-Lease. The Bell Model 14A, like the P-400 armed with a 20 mm cannon, was known as the P-39D-1-BE. The 336 aircraft of this type used four .30-caliber machine guns in place of the .303-caliber guns of the P-400. The Model 14A-1, the P-39D-2-BE, was built on contract AC156 and used a 1,325 hp V-1710-63 (E6) engine. Most of these aircraft went to the Soviet Union, but a few were used by the US with the 347th and 31st Fighter Groups.

The P-39D started as a modification of the original P-39C order in which the two .30-caliber machine guns were removed from the nose, and two .30-caliber machine guns were installed in each wing, with a concurrent reinforcement of the wing structure. Other improvements included self-sealing fuel tanks and a centerline bomb or drop-tank rack. Here, a disarmed P-39D of the 8th Pursuit Group participates in the 1941 Carolina Maneuvers; the red cross was a temporary marking signifying that the aircraft was assigned to the Red Force. The centerline rack is visible below the fuselage. *Stan Piet collection*

A factory-fresh P-39D shows just a slight amount of exhaust staining from its twelve stubs; some P-39Ds had the twelve-stub exhausts rather than the six-stub variant. The fillet between the fuselage and the lower front of the vertical fin was now a standard feature. *National Museum of the United States Air Force*

This P-39D has six stubs per exhaust and exhibits the national insignia used on US military aircraft up to May 1942. On the rudder, probably applied with chalk, are temporary markings. The sway braces of the centerline bomb rack are visible. *National Museum of the United States Air Force*

A new P-39D is viewed from the front. A close examination of the photograph reveals that although the wing machine guns are not yet installed, the round cutouts for them are present, and they have been plugged. "US ARMY" is painted under the wings. *National Museum of the United States Air Force*

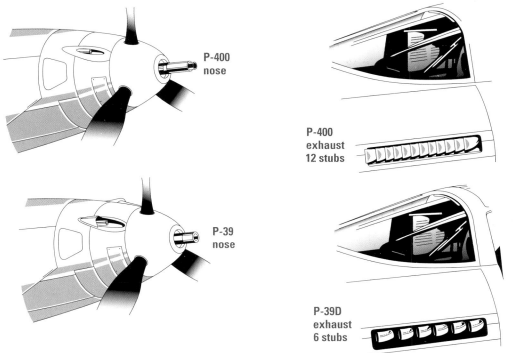

To the left, the P-400 had a 20 mm cannon through the propeller spinner and two .50-caliber machine guns in the nose. P-39Ds had a 37 mm cannon and two .50-caliber machine guns in the nose. To the right, the P-400 had twelve exhaust stubs per side, while the P-39 D had six stubs on each side.

P-400 nose

P-39 nose

P-400 exhaust 12 stubs

P-39D exhaust 6 stubs

In a posed photo, a fully equipped pilot prepares to enter the cockpit of an early P-39 while armorers arrange belts of ammunition. The panel at the top of the gun bay has been removed, but the right-side access panel for the gun bay remains in place. *Stan Piet collection*

P-39Ds of the 39th Pursuit Squadron, 31st Pursuit Group, are lined up at Selfridge Field in 1941. The first plane in line was P-39D-BE, serial number 41-6743; it would be condemned in March 1944. The name of the pilot, written on the black rectangle to the front of the door, appears to be Lt. McCumber. On the door is the insignia of the 39th Pursuit Squadron "Cobras," a cobra rearing its head among some clouds. Bell used several shades of green paint to coat the landing gear and landing-gear bays of P-39s; the paint on the landing-gear struts and retracting links of these P-39s appears to be the same Olive Drab applied to the exteriors of the airplanes. *Stan Piet collection*

A ground crewman helps a pilot into the cockpit of a P-39D assigned to the 31st Pursuit Group. On the door is the insignia of the 40th Pursuit Squadron, the "Fight'n Red Devils," showing a red devil clutching a lightning bolt, with a cloud in the background. *National Museum of the United States Air Force*

Ground crewmen fuel P-39Ds of the 40th Pursuit Squadron, 31st Pursuit Group. The white crosses the planes are wearing signified that they belonged to Blue Force during the Carolina Maneuvers in the fall of 1941. The propeller spinners were yellow. *American Aviation Historical Society*

The lower part of the instrument panel of a P-39D is observed, with the front of the pilot's seat to the bottom and, just forward of it, the bottom of the control stick and its boot. Above the left rudder pedal is the rear end of the left .50-caliber machine gun. The right .50-caliber machine gun is on the other side of the instrument panel, partially hidden by the device to the top right. Directly below the instrument panel is the radio control panel, with three tuning dials. Just below the radio control panel are the 37 mm cannon shell loader handle, the 37 mm shell charger handle, and the engine primer pump knob. *National Museum of the United States Air Force*

The cockpit of a P-39D is viewed through the right door. To the far left is the throttle quadrant, which also holds the fuel mixture control and the propeller control. To the front of the quadrant is the auxiliary switch box, which also held spare fuses. Above that box is the indicator for the positions of the flaps and landing gear, above which are landing-gear and landing-flap switches and a cockpit light. The bare-metal grip above the center of the photo is the charging handle for the left .50-caliber machine gun. A similar charging handle is to the right of the instrument panel. To the front of the control stick boot is the bomb release. *National Museum of the United States Air Force*

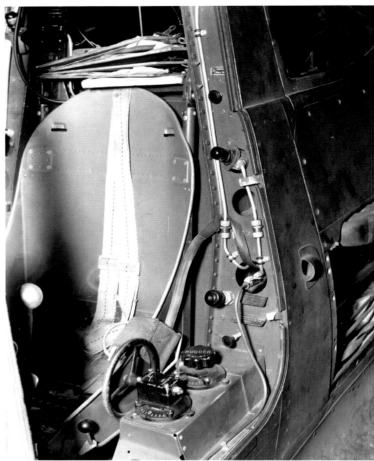

In a view through the left door, to the left is the throttle quadrant. The longer lever on the quadrant is the throttle control. The shorter lever next to it is the fuel mixture control lever. Instruments housed in the instrument panel included but were not limited to a compass, altimeter, turn-and-bank indicator, turn and climb indicators, tachometer, airspeed indicator, radiator and carburetor thermometers, clock, and oil-pressure gauge. The box to the upper right housed a centigrade thermometer, probably for testing purposes. The small box on the sidewall forward of the lower corner of the door was a foot starter switch. *National Museum of the United States Air Force*

The pilot's seat, seat belt, and safety harness are viewed through the left door. On the console at the bottom of the door are, *front to rear*, the trim tab control box and the rudder trim tab control knob. The spoked wheel on the side of the console is the control wheel for the elevator trim tab. The fuselage frame unit inside which the seat is positioned constituted a rollover structure that protected the pilot should the aircraft roll over on the ground. Within the rollover structure above the seat, typically a piece of armored glass was inserted, to protect the pilot's head from the rear and also provide him with visibility to the rear. *National Museum of the United States Air Force*

The right side of the pilot's seat is viewed facing downward. The hand crank to the front of the seat is the landing-gear emergency crank. The small hand crank on the floor to the side of the seat operated the radiator shutter. The large D ring on the floor is the landing-gear clutch. *National Museum of the United States Air Force*

In a view of the cockpit through the left door, to the front of the seat is the boot over the bottom of the control stick, with a zipper so it can be removed. On the front face of the console is the aileron trim tab control; to the front of it is the fuel selector switch. *National Museum of the United States Air Force*

Bell P-39D-1-BE, serial number 41-28360, presents a heavily weathered appearance. The P-39D-1-BE differed from the P-39D-BE in that it had a 20 mm cannon in the nose. The white number 253 had been applied over an older, yellow aircraft number. *Stan Piet collection*

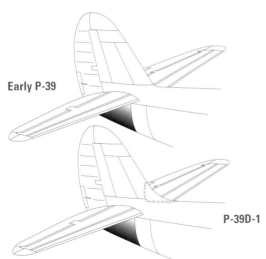

Early P-39

P-39D-1

Airacobras up through the P-39D-BE model had a sharp, angular joint between the lower leading edge of the vertical fin and the top of the fuselage. From the P-39D-1-BE to the end of production of the Airacobras, a fillet was installed at that joint, and some earlier Airacobras were retrofitted with the fillet.

While based with the 55th Fighter Squadron at Charlotte, North Carolina, in July 1942, this Bell P-39D-1-BE, serial number 41-38309, suffered a landing accident. Less than a year later, the plane crashed near Fort Myers, Florida, in May 1943; the pilot bailed out. *Stan Piet collection*

A quartet of Airacobras, including at least two P-39D-1-BEs in the foreground, fly in formation in 1942. The first plane, serial number 41-28360, was seen flying alone in a photograph earlier in this book. The next plane in line is serial number 41-38276. *Stan Piet collection*

Two P-39Ds with the 8P tail code of the 8th Pursuit Group bear red crosses, indicating that they are part of the Red Force in the 1941 Carolina Maneuvers. The individual aircraft numbers are painted in yellow on the tails and the leading edges of the wings. *Stan Piet collection*

This Bell P-39D-1-BE, serial number 41-28277, crashed near Paine Field, Washington, on October 24, 1942. The pilot, 2Lt. James O. Woodruff Jr., was killed in the crash. Because of the extensive nature of the damage, the plane was written off. *National Archives*

The cockpit of P-39D-1-BE, serial number 41-28277, is shown close-up after the fatal crash. In this case, the rollover structure came through unscathed and is visible to the left, with the rear of the canopy having become detached from the fuselage to the lower left. *National Archives*

This Bell Aircraft factory photo depicts a P-39D around early 1942. This is one of the D-model Airacobras, with twelve exhaust stubs on each side and a 37 mm cannon. Below the plane, a 75-gallon auxiliary fuel tank is shackled to the bomb/drop-tank rack. *National Archives*

P-39D-1-BE, serial number 41-38271, has the 20 mm cannon that was a characteristic of that submodel. Protective, light-colored wrappings are around the cannon barrel and .30-caliber machine gun barrels on the wing, and the ports for the .50-caliber machine guns are covered. *National Archives*

A pilot clad in a shearling winter flying jacket, shearling trousers, winter flying helmet, goggles, and oxygen mask clambers up onto the wing of a P-39 Airacobra. The blue of the national insignia virtually fades into the Olive Drab of the fuselage. *Stan Piet collection*

P-39D-1-BE, serial number 41-38350, was piloted by Lt. Irving A. Erickson of the 35th Fighter Squadron, 8th Fighter Group, Fifth Air Force, based at Milne Bay, New Guinea, in 1942. Erickson was awarded the Distinguished Flying Cross for "extraordinary heroism" while serving with the 35th Fighter Squadron in 1943.

A photograph dated November 11, 1941, shows, among a line of Airacobras at an airfield, a P-39D-1-BE marked with the number 10 on the nose and on the rudder, with a Mk. 21 smoke-dispenser tank shackled to the centerline of the belly. Smoke dispensers were used to lay down smoke to mask movements of aircraft, ships, and so forth.

This photo of P-39D-1-BE, serial number 41-38392, was taken at an airfield on Guadalcanal around early 1943. A flexible boot is fitted over the normally exposed bare-metal part of the oleo strut, to protect it from dirt and mud. A 20 mm cannon is mounted in the nose. *National Archives*

Two Airacobras are parked in sandbagged revetments at the airfield of the 2nd Air Base Group near Reykjavík, Iceland, in 1942. The plane on the left exhibits the early-war national insignia with the red circle in the middle of the white star. *National Museum of the United States Air Force*

	XP-39	XP-39B	YP-39	P-39C	P-400	P-39D	P-39D-1, -2	P-39F	P-39J	P-39K	P-39L	P-39M	P-39N	P-39Q
Cannon	none fitted	none fitted	1 × 37 mm	1 × 37 mm	1 × 20 mm	1 × 37 mm	1 × 20 mm M1 or 37 mm	1 × 37 mm	1 × 37 mm	1 × 37 mm	1 × 37 mm	1 × 37 mm	1 × 37 mm	1 × 37 mm
Machine gun	none fitted	none fitted	2 × .50 cal. + 2 × .30 cal.	2 × .50 cal. + 2 × .30 cal.	2 × .50 cal. + 4 × .30 cal.	2 × .50 cal. + 4 × .30 cal.	2 × .50 cal. + 4 × .30 cal.	2 × .50 cal. + 4 × .30 cal.	2 × .50 cal. + 4x .30 cal.	2 × .50 cal. + 4 × .30 cal.	2 × .50 cal. + 4 × .30 cal.	2 × .50 cal. + 4 × .30 cal.	2 × .50 cal. + 4 × .30 cal.	4 × .50 cal.
Bombload	none	none	none	none		500 lbs.	500 lbs.							
Allison engine	V-1710-17, E2	V-1710-37, E5	V-1710-37, E5	V-1710-35 E4	V-1710-35 E4	V-1710-35 E4	V-1710-35 E4 or -63 E6	V-1710-35 E4	V-1710-59 E12	V-1710-63 E6	V-1710-63 E6	V-1710-67 E8 or -83 E18	V-1710-85 E19	V-1710-85 E19
Horsepower	1,150	1,090	1,090	1,150	1,150	1,150	1,150 (-35) or 1,325 (-63)	1,150	1,100	1,325	1,325	1,200	1,200	1,200
Max. speed	390 mph @ 20,000 ft.	375 mph @ 15,000 ft.	368 @ 13,000 ft.	379 mph @ 13,000 ft.	355 mph @ 13,000 ft.	368 mph @ 12,000 ft.	368 mph @ 12,000 ft.				360 mph @ 15,000 ft.	370 mph @ 15,000 ft.	379 mph @ 10,000 ft.	385 mph @ 15,000 ft.
Cruise speed														
Service ceiling	32,000 ft.	36,000 ft.	33,300 ft.	33,200 ft.	24,000 ft.	32,100 ft.	32,100 ft.						38,500 ft.	35,000 ft.
Combat range		1,400 miles	600 miles	450 miles		800 miles	800 miles						750 miles	650 miles
Wingspan	35 ft., 10 in.	34 ft.	34 ft.	34 ft.		34 ft.	34 ft.			34 ft.	34 ft.		34 ft.	34 ft.
Length	28 ft., 8 in.	29 ft., 9 in.	30 ft., 2 in.	30 ft., 2 in.		30 ft., 2 in.	30 ft., 2 in.		30 ft., 2 in.	30 ft., 2 in.			30 ft., 2 in.	30 ft., 2 in.
Height	11 ft.	9 ft., 3 in.	11 ft., 10 in.	11 ft., 10 in.		11 ft., 10 in.	11 ft., 10 in.		11 ft., 10 in.	11 ft., 10 in.			12 ft., 5 in.	12 ft., 5 in.
Empty weight	3,995 lbs.	4,955 lbs.	5,042 lbs.	5,070 lbs.		6,300 lbs.	6,300 lbs.			6,300 lbs.	6,300 lbs.		5,675 lbs.	5,645 lbs.
Gross weight	5,550 lbs.	5,834 lbs.	7,180 lbs.	7,180 lbs.		7,830 lbs.	7,830 lbs.			7,830 lbs.	7,830 lbs.		7,800 lbs.	7,700 lbs.
Max. gross weight	6,204 lbs.	6,450 lbs.	7,235 lbs.	7,305 lbs.		8,200 lbs.	8,200 lbs.			8,200 lbs.	9,100 lbs.		8,200 lbs.	8,300 lbs.
Number built/converted	1	1	13	20	675	60	864	231	25	210	250	240	2,095	4,905
Serial numbers	38-326	38-326	40-027 through 40-039	40-2971 through 40-3050	AH570 through AH739 AP264 through AP384 BW100 through BW183 BX135 through BX434	40-2991 through 40-3050 41-6722 through 40-7115	41-28257 through 41-28406 41-38220 through 41-38404 41-38405 through 41-38562 41-38563	41-7116 through 41-7344	41-7043 through 41-7056 41-7059 through 41-7079	42-4244 through 42-4453l35	42-4454 through 42-4703	42-4704 through 42-4943	42-4944 through 42-5043 42-8727 through 42-9726 42-18246 through 2-19240	42-20546 through 42-21250 44-2001 through 44-3000 44-3001 through 44-4000 44-32167 through 44-32666 44-70905 through 44-71504

This Airacobra, serial number 41-19502, was the second of the three XP-39E-BE experimental aircraft that Bell Aircraft produced. That company designated them the Model 23 and intended that they be used to test an installation of the Continental V-1430-1 supercharged inverted-V engine. These planes were not armed, and light-colored fairings were applied over the gunports on the nose. The wingtips were flattened. *National Museum of the United States Air Force*

In order to improve the Airacobra's performance, and perhaps return some of the high-altitude capabilities called for in the original X-609 Circular Proposal, on April 10, 1941, contract AC18373 was issued. Under this contract, two P-39D airframes were modified to accommodate the Continental V-1430-1 engine. This inverted V, expected to develop 2,100 hp, was a definite improvement over the V-1710 Allison used in the P-39D. A third airframe for static testing was soon added to the initial order.

In contrast to the base P-39D airframe, these airframes had a new, longer wing with square-cut wingtips. To fit the larger engine, the fuselage was extended by 21 inches.

Bell assigned number 23 to the new-type model, known to the military as the XP-39E, and work proceeded. But by the time the airframes were completed, the Continental had fallen behind schedule, and the Army opted instead to install a 1,325 hp Allison

V-1710-47 engine with two-stage supercharger. Empty and loaded weights rose to 6,936 and 8,918 pounds, respectively, making the XP-39E the heaviest Airacobra.

The first XP-39E, serial number 41-19501, made its maiden flight on February 21, 1942. It could climb to 20,000 feet in 9.3 minutes, and it reached a maximum speed of 386 miles per hour at 21,680 feet. Regrettably, that aircraft crashed less than a month later, but fortunately pilot Bob Stanley parachuted to safety.

The second prototype, serial number 41-19502, first flew on April 4, 1942, and the decision was made to convert the static-test article, serial 41-71464, to flying configuration. Test performance was so impressive that the aircraft was redesignated XP-76, and 4,000 production models were ordered. Although this order was later canceled, many of the lessons learned in this program were incorporated in the P-63 Kingcobra.

Bell XP-39E-BE, serial number 41-19502, is viewed from the front. The vertical tails of each of the three XP-39E-BEs were different, with this one being flat on the top. A recessed landing light is visible on the leading edge of the left wing. No armament was installed in the plane. *National Archives*

The vertical stabilizer and rudder of the second XP-39E-BE were not a reworking of the existing P-39 structures but entirely new structures. The fuselage was lengthened by 1.75 feet to accommodate the new engine, and the wingtips were nearly straight. *American Aviation Historical Society*

High-performance aircraft propellers are complicated precision pieces of equipment in their own right. The US entry into World War II and the increased demand for military equipment pushed the nation's manufacturing capability to the limit, including those for propellers. Production Airacobras to this point had been equipped with Curtiss Electric propellers. With Curtiss unable to meet the demand, Bell adapted the Airacobra to use a constant-speed Aeroproducts propeller. The new model, which but for the propeller was almost identical to the P-39D, was known internally as the Model 15B, and to the military it was the P-39F.

Contract AC-15675, issued on September 13, 1940, was for 229 of the aircraft. Externally, the most immediately noticeable difference between the P-39D and P-39F was the presence on most P-39Fs of twelve exhaust stacks, versus the six exhaust stubs found on the P-39D.

Internally, other changes began to take place. Colt was unable to keep up with the demand for the M4 37 mm cannon (contrary to some assertions, the P-39 did not use an American Armaments gun). To augment Colt production, in January 1942, Oldsmobile Division of General Motors also contracted to build the 37 mm M4. Oldsmobile began M4 production in August 1942 and halted it at the end of July 1943. Colt continued to build the guns until November 1943. Although originally Olds had been contracted for 6,195 guns, only 2,779 were built before the contract was terminated. Colt, on the other hand, built 8,667.

Airacobras saw action in the Aleutian Islands in World War II. This photo of ground crewmen servicing a P-39F of the 54th Fighter Group at Adak portrays a good idea of the harsh weather conditions the aircrews encountered in the Aleutians, where fog, heavy precipitation, and freezing cold predominated during much of the year. The fuselage panels around the Allison V-1710-35 engine, fitted with twelve exhaust stubs per side, have been removed, exposing the power plant to view. An armorer next to the removed rear half of the canopy replenishes a .50-caliber ammunition box. The Aeroproducts propeller, 10 feet, 4 inches in diameter, now replaced the Curtiss Electric propeller. *Stan Piet collection*

Bell P-39F-1-BE Airacobra, serial number 41-7246, was fitted with six exhaust stubs per side and flash suppressors for the nose-mounted .50-caliber machine guns. An armor plate abuts the bottom of the windshield. A sealant apparently is on the wing guns. *National Museum of the United States Air Force*

The same P-39F-1-BE in the preceding photo is viewed from the side. "Wright Field" is stenciled to the front of the pilot's door. What appears to be a stub mast is aft of the carburetor air scoop. A gunsight is visible through the side of the windshield. *National Museum of the United States Air Force*

Bell P-39F-1-BE, serial number 41-7246, is seen in a left-rear three-quarters view. A screen with a frame is positioned slightly forward of the front of the carburetor air scoop, to keep out foreign objects. On the wing near the wing root is a nonskid walkway. *National Museum of the United States Air Force*

This P-39F-1-BE has its tail number (the serial number minus its first digit, 4) on both the tail and the forward fuselage. On the side of the fuselage aft of the national insignia is a nonstandard fixture with a bulge set at an angle; its purpose is uncertain. *National Museum of the United States Air Force*

Only twenty P-39Fs were built after this example, which is flying from Foster Field, Texas. Faintly visible here are the antenna lead, stretching from the rudder to the fuselage, and the red surround to the national insignia. *National Museum of the United States Air Force*

The upper instrument panel of P-39F 41-7246 appears to have been finished in a black crackle finish paint, while the center portion of the instrumeant panel was evidently finished in matte black. *National Museum of the United States Air Force*

In the Aleutians, a mechanic services the engine of P-39F-1-BE, serial number 41-7341, of the 57th Fighter Squadron, 54th Fighter Group, in July 1942. The wolf's head was the unofficial symbol of the squadron. This Airacobra was condemned in October 1942. *National Museum of the United States Air Force*

Aircraft collector Jerry Yagen contracted with Pioneer Aero Ltd., of Ardmore, New Zealand, to restore this Airacobra to flying condition. The basis for the restoration was the P-39F with serial number 41-2175, which served with the US 36th Fighter Squadron, 8th Fighter Group, in Australia in 1942. The plane was damaged in a gear-up landing in May 1942, and the remains of the airframe were recovered thirty years later. *Rich Kolasa*

On each propeller blade of the Yagen Airacobra are logo decals for Curtiss Electric Propellers. The flange of the light-colored sleeve for the 37 mm cannon muzzle is fastened to the propeller spinner with four screws. Details of the nose landing gear are in view. *Rich Kolasa*

On the left side of the fuselage to the rear of the engine compartment is an access door to the radio compartment. The door is secured with camloc (also called Dzus) fasteners and has a piano hinge on the bottom. Above that door is a smaller access door, with two camloc fasteners and a piano hinge on the bottom. *Rich Kolasa*

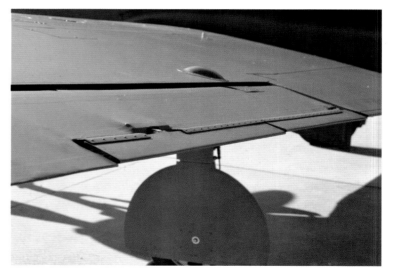

The ailerons (the left one is depicted) were constructed of fabric over metal ribs attached to an Alclad beam. On the inboard side of each of the ailerons was a pilot-controlled trim tab, made of phenolic plastic. On the outboard side of each aileron trim tab was a servo tab, also made of plastic. The servo tab was automatically actuated at a neutral 2 degrees above the thrust line of the aircraft. The yellow object in the center background is the pop-up indicator for the left landing gear. *Rich Kolasa*

The right cockpit door, cockpit canopy, and right engine cowling panels are depicted. The yellow object to the right is the pop-up indicator for the nose landing gear. The pilot used this indicator to ascertain that the gear was fully extended before attempting a landing. Similar indicators for the main landing gear were on each wing. *Rich Kolasa*

The rudder, as viewed from the right rear, is turned to the left. It was made of fabric over a metal framework, with formed aluminum-sheet covers over the top and the bottom. The trim tab was made of plastic. The elevators were of fabric over metal-frame construction. *Rich Kolasa*

Details of the wing fillet, the carburetor-air scoop, the right engine cowling and cockpit door, and the cockpit canopy are in view. On the wing toward the right is the right landing-gear pop-up indicator. *Rich Kolasa*

The Airacobra in the collection of Jerry Yagen is shown with an Olive Drab over Neutral Gray camouflage scheme, and with markings to represent P-39Q-5-BE, serial number 42-20341, a plane that actually was sent to the Soviets under the Lend-Lease program. *Rich Kolasa*

The P-39J varied from the P-39F by having the Allison V-1710-59 engine. Only twenty-five aircraft were designated the P-39J. This particular aircraft was shown as having been declared surplus on January 9, 1945, and sent to Reconstruction Finance Corporation in Ponca City, Oklahoma. *San Diego Air & Space Museum*

This P-39J, serial number 41-7073, was the aircraft of Lt. Leslie Spoonts of the 57th Fighter Squadron, in the Aleutian Islands from June to December 1942. Three kill markings for Japanese aircraft are to the front of the door, and what appears to be sealant tape has been applied to the sides of the doors. This plane was from a block of Airacobras originally assigned P-39D-BE serial numbers, redesignated P-39Fs, but finally designated P-39Js. *National Museum of the United States Air Force*

CHAPTER 9
P-39K

The P-39K was part of the so-called "midseries" Airacobras, which originally constituted the P-39G order. This order was canceled and broken up into four new models: the P-39K, P-39L, P-39M, and P-39N. Bell P-39K, serial number 42-4395, one of the 210 Airacobras of that model, casts its shadow on an airfield tarmac. A belly tank is installed under the fuselage. An air vent is visible below and aft of the machine-gun port on the nose. On the other side of this plane is Bell P-39N-1-BE, serial number 42-18430. *Bill Pippin collection*

On August 21, 1941, the US Army Air Forces—as the Army Air Corps had become on June 20 of that year—ordered 1,800 copies of the Bell Model 26, which was designated the P-39G. This was the largest Airacobra order yet placed; in fact, it was the largest aircraft order placed with Bell up to this time.

The P-39Gs, assigned serial numbers 42-4244 through 42-5043 and 42-8727 through 42-9726, were to be essentially P-39D-2s, except utilizing Aeroproducts propellers rather than Curtiss Electric propellers.

However, none of P-39Gs were actually built. As the Army Air Force requested more and more changes on the basis of combat experience and component availability, the aircraft on the large order were broken down into smaller groups.

While in later years a production block suffix to the aircraft model number system began to be used (such as P-39Q-30-BE), such was not the case in 1941–42. Thus, changes in the aircraft begat entirely new model designations.

The first group spawned from the P-39G was the P-39K, and these were assigned serial numbers 42-4244 through 42-4453. The P-39K was powered by an Allison V-1710-63 (E6), which boosted horsepower to 1,325, compared to the P-39J's 1,100. Six exhaust stacks protruded from each side of the fuselage. Six of the P-39Ks were modified for photoreconnaissance work, with two cameras installed in the aft fuselage. These aircraft were designated P-39K-2-BE.

Seen here is P-39K, serial number 42-4383. This model featured the Allison V-1710-63 engine, rated at 1,325 hp, and an Aeroproducts propeller. Armament included a 37 mm cannon and two .50-caliber machine guns in the nose and two .30-caliber machine guns in each wing. Ammunition storage for each .50-caliber machine gun was increased by fifteen rounds. The number 83 was painted on the nose of this example. *National Museum of the United States Air Force*

Personnel of the 29th Air Service Group inspect a P-39K. Flash suppressors are present on the blast tubes for the .50-caliber machine guns in the nose. Without the flash suppressors installed, firing the .50-caliber guns in the darkness could temporarily blind the pilot. *National Archives*

CHAPTER 10

P-39L

P-39L-1-BE, serial number 42-4563, rests at the edge of a field. The P-39L, of which 250 were delivered, had the same Allison V-1710-63 engine as the P-39K but had the Curtiss Electric propeller instead of the Aeroproducts propeller. This engine provided improved low-altitude performance over the Allison V-1710-35 engine of the P-39D and P-39D-1-BE. Two prominent new features with the P-39L that continued on subsequent models of the P-39 were a large vent on each side of the nose, to expel fumes from the guns, and a redesigned nosewheel with a larger diameter and better aerodynamics.
American Aviation Historical Society

The 1,800-plane P-39G order was ultimately broken down into four other models, P-39K through P-39N, collectively referred to as midseries aircraft by enthusiasts. The second type to be derived from the P-39G order was the P-39L. The 36,000 employees at Bell's Wheatfield, New York, plant, which was located in the Buffalo / Niagara Falls area, turned out 250 P-39Ls. While some of these aircraft were supplied to the Soviet Union, others were used by USAAF units, which took them into combat in New Guinea and North Africa during 1943.

The P-39L continued to use the Allison V-1710-63 (E6) as found on the P-39K, but the propeller reverted to a Curtiss Electric model, rather than the K's Aeroproducts. Experience from the field dictated some changes to the Airacobra effective with this model. The first of these was a change to the forward landing gear. While the outside diameter of the front tire remained the same, the diameter of the metal nosewheel increased, meaning that a tire with a lower sidewall was used. This style offered less drag on takeoff than the prior design.

Also, to address complaints that gases from guns in the nose would fill the cockpit, triangular vents were added to each side of the nose. These vents, as well as the revised nosewheel, would be features on all further Airacobra production. Provision was also made for the mounting of rocket rails under the wing. The serial numbers assigned to the P-39L were 42-4454 through 42-4703. Eleven of these aircraft were converted into photoreconnaissance aircraft that were designated P-39L-2-BE, each equipped for the installation of two cameras. The serials of the camera-equipped planes were 42-4457, 4461, 4462, 4465, 4466, 4470, 4471, 4476, 4489, 4553, and 4630.

On a winter day, a ground crewman sticks his head through the side window of P-39L-1-BE, serial number 42-4673. The enlarged nosewheel is visible; the tire's sidewall height was reduced, so the overall diameter of the tire remained unchanged from previous models. *National Museum of the United States Air Force*

P-39D

P-39Q

As opposed to the nose of early P-39s, *left*, an air vent was added to Airacobras below and to the rear of the machine-gun port on each side of the nose, starting with the P-39Ls. The bottom illustration shows the .50-caliber machine gun pod added under each wing, starting with the P-39Q. These detachable pods replaced the two .30-caliber machine guns in each wing.

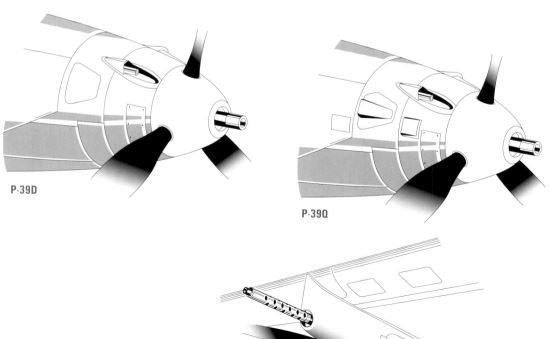

Gun Pod

A Bell P-39L cockpit is viewed through the right door. On the inside of the left door are the door-operating handle on the top forward corner, and, *at the center*, the window-operating handle. The bottom of the clear-view window is at the top center.

A mechanic poses next to the open door of an Airacobra. The triangular fume vent on the side of the nose was standardized with the P-39L but apparently retrofitted on some earlier-model P-39s. Another feature introduced with the midseries P-39s was the clear-view window panel on the left side of the windshield, which could be opened to give the pilot an unobstructed view forward should the windshield get covered with ice, condensation, or oil. On the inside of the door is the flight report holder and map case. Members of the Women's Auxiliary Army Corps (WAAC), or, after 1943, the Women's Army Corps (WAC), contributed significantly to the war effort, with many employed in maintaining and servicing aircraft. *Stan Piet collection*

The cockpit of a P-39L is seen through the left door. To the left is the throttle quadrant. Above the top of the control stick, the bottom of the gunsight is visible. Written on the flap of the map case on the left door are instructions for landing-gear and landing-flap operation.

A passing plane shot this photo of factory-fresh Airacobras lined up at an airfield, most likely at Bell Aircraft, judging by the men in business suits on the tarmac. The tail numbers on the planes reflect serial numbers all within the range for P-39Ls; the tail number comprised the serial number less the first digit. Hence, on the right side of the tarmac, the visible tail numbers, 24663, 24677, 24660, and 24668, translate to serial numbers 42-4663, 42-4677, 42-4660, and 42-4668. The first two digits of the serial number, in this case 42, indicated the year in which the aircraft was contracted. *National Museum of the United States Air Force*

While it was a training aircraft for pilots destined for the 357th Fighter Group, P-39L 42-4687 collided in midair with a towed target and crashed at Half Moon Bay, California, on August 28, 1943. In September it was classified CL-26 (nonairworthy) and relegated to a being static-training aircraft for USAAF maintenance personnel at Hamilton Airfield, California. The pilot in the crash, Capt. Fletcher E. Adams, survived that incident and went on to score nine aerial victories while flying with the 362nd Fighter Squadron before being killed in action on May 30, 1944. The aircraft had a white empennage and nose band and a camouflage scheme of Olive Drab over Neutral Gray.

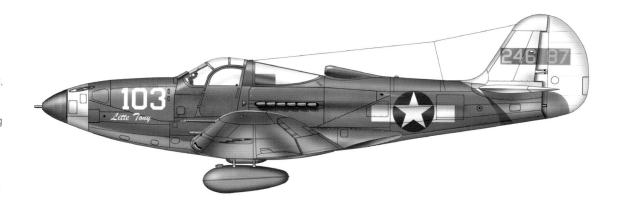

The crewman at center adjusts a photoreconnaissance camera mounted in the lower fuselage of an Airacobra, while the man to the left holds another camera. Beginning with the P-39D, some examples of each model were modified for photoreconnaissance. *Stan Piet collection*

Two cameras are shown in their bay in the bottom of the fuselage of an Airacobra, just behind the trailing edges of the wings. The aft camera (*the closer of the two in this photo*) pointed downward, while the forward camera pointed obliquely to the rear. *National Museum of the United States Air Force*

A sheet of plywood has been leaned against a set of steps in the background to help highlight the profile of the camera fairing on the bottom of the fuselage of a photoreconnaissance Airacobra. From this angle, the fairing looks like a small air scoop. *National Museum of the United States Air Force*

A K-25 oblique camera (*left*) and a K-24 vertical camera (*right*) are shown in a P-39L-2-BE, the photo-recon version of the P-39L. The power rating of the K-25 camera, 24 volts, is stenciled on the lens case, and the power cable for the camera is visible. *National Museum of the United States Air Force*

The K-25 (*left*) and K-24 cameras for a P-39 installation are depicted on their mounting rack. Stenciled on the cross-member of the frame to the left is "upper fwd." The pilot operated the cameras through a small switch box forward of his left-side console. *National Museum of the United States Air Force*

The bay to the rear of the engine in a camera-equipped Airacobra is viewed from above, with the rear of the bay to the top of the photo. Toward the top is the radiator coolant expansion tank; below it is the top of a K-24 vertical camera. *National Museum of the United States Air Force*

Beginning in November 1942 the third group of aircraft derived from the P-39G order—the P-39M—began to leave the Bell production line. Production of the P-39M totaled 240 aircraft, with these Airacobras assigned the serial numbers 42-4704 through 42-4943.

The P-39M differed from the P-39L in that a different engine was used. The P-39L's V-1710-63 was set aside for a new power plant, with the intent of sacrificing some low-altitude performance in order to gain better high-altitude performance. The engine used initially in the P-39M was the Allison V-1710-67 (E8). Later the V-1710-83 (E18) was used. In either case, a Curtiss Electric propeller was used. The engine change gave the P-39M a 10-mile-per-hour edge over its predecessor at 15,000 feet.

As was the case with the two prior models, a handful of aircraft were modified for reconnaissance. In this case, eight aircraft, which were redesignated P-39M-BE-2, were equipped for mounting two cameras each. As with the earlier photo Airacobras, the armament was retained. The serial numbers of the camera-equipped P-39Ms were 42-4704 through 42-4706, 42-4710, 42-4712, 42-4751, 42-4795, and 42-4824.

The P-39M, another midseries Airacobra, was similar to the P-39L, but with an Allison V-1710-67 (E8) engine in early-production examples and the Allison V-1710-83 (E18) engine in some later examples and as a retrofit. The propeller once again was by Aeroproducts. The P-39M could achieve a speed of 370 miles per hour at an altitude of 15,000 feet, a 10-mile-per-hour advantage over the P-39L at the same altitude. The first examples of the P-39M were produced in November 1942, and a total of 240 were built. Seen here is P-39M, serial number 42-4770. *National Museum of the United States Air Force*

The cockpit of the P-39M is depicted. The .50-caliber machine guns have been removed from the nose; their butts and charging handles normally would appear on each side of the center panel of the instrument panel. At the top of the instrument panel is an optical gunsight, fitted with a crash pad to protect the pilot's head should it strike the sight. On the left side of the windshield is the clear-view window, with two small hinges visible on its right side. On the clear-view window's left side was a small lock and catch. *National Museum of the United States Air Force*

Airacobras line the Alexandria
Army Air Field, Alexandria,
Louisiana, on March 8, 1943. All
the visible tail numbers of the
aircraft in the row to the right mark
them as P-39M-1-BEs. The first
one, 42-4813, was condemned on
August 10, 1943. *National Archives*

This P-39M, serial number 42-4734,
crashed on takeoff on a ferrying
flight from USAAF Station 590,
Burtonwood, Britain, on February
18, 1943. The pilot, Walter O. West,
survived, but the plane was
written off. *National Museum of
the United States Air Force*

CHAPTER 12

After production of the P-39K, L, and M, the remaining 1,100 aircraft of the would-be 1,800-plane P-39G order were produced as P-39Ns. Not only that, but a further 1,200 P-39Ns were ordered. Ultimately, 205 of the aircraft on the second order were produced as P-39Qs, leaving 995 of that order as P-39Ns. Combined with the carryover from the P-39G order, the result was 2,095 of the P-39Ns leaving the Bell assembly line. Regardless of contract, all P-39Ns were built with the V-1710-85 (E19) engine.

This engine differed from the -83 used in the P-39M by incorporating a different propeller reduction gear ratio. In front of the engine was an Aeroproducts propeller. That propeller was 10 feet, 4 inches in diameter on the first 166 P-39Ns, after which a propeller 11 feet, 7 inches was used.

In response to a USAAF request, at the same time that the prop diameter was increased, four fuel cells were deleted in order to bring the maximum gross weight down from 9,100 pounds to 8,750 pounds. This change reduced the internal fuel capacity from 120 gallons to 87 gallons, with a corresponding reduction in range. Kits were provided so that units in the field could install the tanks in order to bring fuel capacity back up to 120 gallons in those instances where range was more important than weight. Again, in reference to combat weight, the last 695 P-39Ns built replaced the bulletproof glass behind the pilot with an armored headrest, for a savings of 38 pounds. A total of 163 P-39Ns were adapted for photoreconnaissance.

The P-39N was the first model of Airacobra to be produced in quantities larger than in the hundreds, with a total of 2,095 being delivered. This early-production P-39N, serial number 42-9107, was part of the P-39G order, which was canceled. It had the Aeroproducts propeller with a diameter of 10 feet, 4 inches. After the 166th P-39N, the Aeroproducts 11-foot, 7-inch propeller was substituted. *American Aviation Historical Society*

The first 1,100 P-39Ns were part of the canceled P-39G order that were redesignated P-39Ks, P-39Ls, and P-39Ms; the balance of the P-39Ns represented new contracts. The engine was the Allison V-1710-85 (E19), rated at 1,115 hp at 15,000 feet. Starting with the 167th P-39N, four fuel cells were deleted in order to reduce the gross weight, but this significantly reduced the range, so the cells were sometimes reinstalled in the field when additional range was desired. This aircraft is P-39N-1-BE, serial number 42-9392, nicknamed "Dibbo." *National Museum of the United States Air Force*

"Dibbo," P-39N-1-BE, serial number 42-9392, seen in the preceding photo, is viewed from its right rear. Faintly visible are very faded white bars that had been added to the sides of the blue circle of the national insignia; these were a June 1943 revision to the insignia. *National Museum of the United States Air Force*

Bell P-39N-1-BE, serial number 42-9302, appears in US Army Air Forces markings prior to being sent to the Soviet Union under the Lend-Lease program. Although not visible from this angle, there were six exhaust stubs on each side of the plane. The propeller was by Aeroproducts, with a diameter of 11 feet, 7 inches. *San Diego Air & Space Museum*

A line of Airacobras at Brooks Field, San Antonio, Texas in 1943, include S-26, the fifth-from-last P-39N-1-BE, serial number 42-18541. On the closest aircraft, various details are visible, including the 37 mm muzzle sleeve, nose landing gear, and vents. *National Archives*

In this close look at the instrument panel of a P-39N, the radio control panel is at the bottom center. To the upper left of the radio control panel are the bomb-release handle and starter switch. To the lower left are the throttle quadrant and the photographer's knee. The large instrument to the left is a radio compass, while the instrument in the light-colored holder to the upper right is an accelerometer. *National Museum of the United States Air Force*

P-39N-1, serial number 42-9349, piloted by Albert J. Slimak, crashed on takeoff near Santa Rosa, California, on September 21, 1943. It was damaged beyond repair. Surrounding the 37 mm cannon muzzle at the front of the spinner is a sleeve found on some P-39s. *National Museum of the United States Air Force*

Air Forces personnel pose for their photo on top of a P-39N at Aiken Army Airfield, South Carolina. The pilot's name stenciled below the canopy is illegible, but the crew chief's name, a Sergeant Praither, is present. *San Diego Air & Space Museum*

Pilots stand in front of camera-equipped P-39N-3-BEs of the 71st Reconnaissance Group. Two tail numbers, 28809 and 28836, are visible (serial numbers 42-8809 and 42-8836). Several planes have illegible nicknames on the noses and diagonal bands on the fuselages. *National Museum of the United States Air Force*

The engine of P-39N 42-8878 is being run up while a ground crewman stands ready to use a fire extinguisher if an engine fire breaks out. Some of the contents of the gun bay are visible. *San Diego Air & Space Museum*

A P-39N with serial number 42-8898, assigned to the 18th Fighter Group, awaits its next mission at an airfield on Guadalcanal in June 1943. The plane is severely smeared and splattered with oil and grease, but the markings appear to have been recently repainted. *National Museum of the United States Air Force*

Two three-tube rocket launchers, probably accommodating 4.5-inch rockets, are attached to underwing mounting points on a midseries Airacobra, probably a P-39N. Rockets enabled the Airacobras to take on enemy armor and shipping more effectively. *National Archives*

Rocket-launching tubes are viewed from the side. On a mission over the harbor at Rabaul, P-39s reportedly sank forty Japanese barges with rockets. A disadvantage of the rocket tubes was that they diminished the maximum airspeed of the aircraft. *National Archives*

Crewmen scramble to ready P-39N-5-BE, serial number 42-18794, for a mission. The final 695 P-39Ns were given the -5-BE suffix, and these aircraft eliminated 38 pounds of armor and had an armor steel plate in the rollover structure instead of the armor glass panel. *American Aviation Historical Society*

Capt. George S. Hilbert was the pilot of P-39N-5-BE, serial number 42-18805, assigned to the 41st Fighter Squadron, 35th Fighter Group, 5th Air Force. The nickname "TODDY III" was painted over the exhaust stubs, and pinup art was painted on the door.

A snowbound Airacobra exhibits tail number 24961, indicating this was one of the P-39Ns delivered to the Soviet Union. A dark-colored tarp is loosely draped over much of the fuselage, and a light material is stretched over the wings, to prevent icing. *Library of Congress*

A grinning, decorated Maj. Nikolai I. Proshenkov, Hero of the Soviet Union, sits on the wing of his P-39. An arrow / lightning bolt, pretty girls, and stars, likely recording some of his eventual nineteen aerial victories, decorate Proshenkov's aircraft. *Hans-Heiri Stapfer*

Although the tail number of this Airacobra is partially hidden by the pitot tube, what can be seen of it is consistent with that of a P-39N-1-BE destined for the Soviet Union. Chalked on the gun-bay cover is "N-1-22." *San Diego Air & Space Museum*

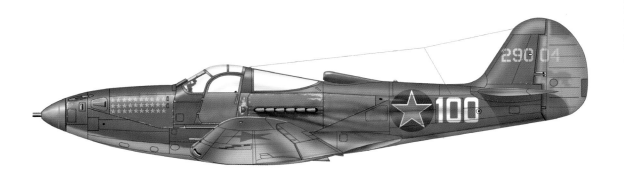

P-39N, serial number 42-9004, was piloted by Capt. Aleksandr Ivanovich Pokryshkin of the 9th Guards Fighter Air Division of the Soviet air force in 1943. The plane had a heavily weathered Olive Drab over Neutral Gray finish, with victory stars on the side of the forward fuselage. Pokryshkin finished the war with forty-eight kills.

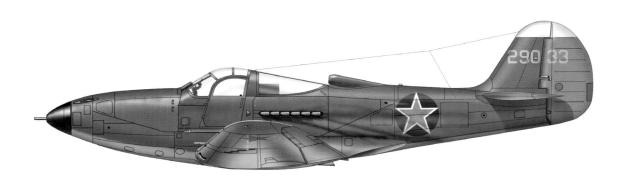

Bell P-39N, serial number 42-9033, was flown by two Soviet aces: Grigoriy Ustinovich Dol'nikov and Capt. Ivan Il'ich Babak, both of the 100th Guards Fighter Air Regiment. The Soviets applied large red stars with white borders over the original USAAF recognition stars.

By 1943, the Free French were acquiring P-39Ns, employing them mainly in maritime patrols. This P-39N, serial number 42-9410, is from Free French Unit GC II/6 "Travail." The national insignia had a red outer ring, white center ring, and blue circle in the center. *National Museum of the United States Air Force*

Ex-USAAF P-39N, serial number 42-9377, served with the Italian Cobelligerent Air Force (Aviazione Cobelligerante Italiana), which fought in cooperation with the Allies. The red, white, and green roundel was superimposed over the US insignia, the bars of which remain. *National Museum of the United States Air Force*

An armorer is making adjustments to the guns of a P-39. The bare-metal box for .50-caliber ammunition has been removed from the gun bay and is resting on the scaffold plank, and a belt of ammunition from it is draped over the rail of the scaffold. *Stan Piet collection*

The Pima Air & Space Museum, Tucson, Arizona, preserves P-39N-5-BE, serial number 42-18814. This Airacobra is thought to have served with the 110th Tactical Reconnaissance Squadron in New Guinea in 1944, and the Military Aircraft Restoration Corporation recovered this airframe from Tadji, New Guinea, in 1972. The plane has been painted to replicate a P-39 serving with the 110th Tactical Reconnaissance Squadron. *Author*

The Pima Air & Space Museum's P-39N has been nicknamed *Girlie* and exhibits pinup art on the right cockpit door. A fairing has been screwed onto the leading edge of the wing, faintly visible to the left of the landing gear, to cover the openings where the barrels of two machine guns originally protruded. *Author*

More P-39Qs were built than all other models combined. Perhaps fittingly, the P-39Q was also the final Airacobra variant, and the 4,905 examples of this type were divided between eight production blocks.

Unlike most other model changes, the P-39Q retained the same engine—the Allison V-1710-85 (E19)—used by its immediate predecessor. Heavily revised, however, was the aircraft's armament. Gone were the pair of .30-caliber machine guns embedded in each wing. With the Q, joining the pair of nose-mounted .50-caliber machine guns—and of course the 37 mm cannon—was a single additional .50-caliber machine gun mounted in a faired pod beneath each wing. This installation was not particularly popular with the Russians, and their aircraft often did not include the underwing guns.

Provision for mounting K-24 and K-25 cameras for photoreconaissance was added to 148 P-39Q-1-BE, those aircraft being reclassified as P-39Q-6-BE. Eight P-39Q-10-BE aircraft were similarly modified, becoming P-39Q-11-BE.

Despite the abundant production, the P-39Q continued to be relatively scarce in USAAF use (as compared to the P-38 and P-47), because nearly half of the P-39Q production was supplied to the Soviets, with further examples provided to the Free French and Italian cobelligerent forces.

The P-39Q-21-BE introduced a four-bladed Aeroproducts propeller in lieu of the previously used three-blade model. It was later determined that the four-blade prop caused directional stability issues with the airframe, and, beginning with the P-39Q-30-BE, the prop reverted to a three-blade model. The bulk of the 109 P-39Q-21-BE and 700 P-39Q-25-BE four-blade-equipped aircraft went to the Soviet Union.

The P-39Q was the last and most numerous model of the Airacobra, with 4,905 being produced. Externally, the most noticeable difference between the P-39Q and the midseries Airacobras was the elimination of the .30-caliber machine guns in the wings in favor of a detachable pod with a .50-caliber machine gun under each wing. Often, the pods were left unmounted. This example, serial number 42-20893, was a Bell P-39Q-10-BE. It crashed into the Atlantic Ocean off St. Catherine Island, Georgia, on September 26, 1943, with Henry V. Walseth at the controls. *Stan Piet collection*

A Bell P-39Q-20-BE displays its front left quarter. The pods for the .50-caliber machine guns are in place. The spinner has the sleeve over the 37 mm cannon muzzle. The wheel cover on the nosewheel is not installed, providing a view of the spoked wheel. *National Museum of the United States Air Force*

The same P-39Q-20-BE seen in the preceding photograph is viewed from the left side. The pitot tube projects from the wing above the .50-caliber underwing machine gun. Radio equipment is visible under the rear of the cockpit canopy. *National Museum of the United States Air Force*

The front profiles of the underwing machine gun pods are visible on this late P-39Q-20-BE. Some sources state that these pods were deleted from this and all following submodels of the P-39Q, but the pods obviously are present on this example. *National Museum of the United States Air Force*

PARKING HARNESS--CONTROL STICK AND RUDDER.
P-39 Q-10-BE
8/15/43
32079

This photo illustrates the installation of a lock for the control stick, termed the parking harness, on a P-39Q. It comprised a tubular bar that attached to mounts on the front of each door opening, and a clamp that held the grip of the stick stationary. *National Museum of the United States Air Force*

The throttle quadrant and linkages are visible on the left side of a P-39Q cockpit. Considerable paint is already worn off those linkages, although the plane appears to be brand new. *National Museum of the United States Air Force*

The instrument panel of the P-39Q is similar in layout to the instrument panels of preceding models of the Airacobra, but the console below the instrument panel has a different design in this example, including a faceplate around the radio controls. *National Museum of the United States Air Force*

An armor plate, visible through the triangular opening, serves to protect the engine accessories to the rear of the engine in this August 1943 view of the engine compartment from the right side of a P-39Q. At the bottom center is the right landing-flap motor. *National Museum of the United States Air Force*

ENGINE ACCESSORY ARMOR PLATE INSTALLED.

P-39 Q-10-BE   8/15/43
                           32086

The engine-accessory armor plate is viewed from the left side of a P-39Q. The Allison engine and several of the exhaust stubs are visible to the left. The wing and fillet have been removed, showing the outer edge of the center wing section to the lower left. *National Museum of the United States Air Force*

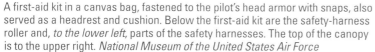

RELOCATED FIRST AID KIT

P-39Q-15-BE   9/30/43
36219

A first-aid kit in a canvas bag, fastened to the pilot's head armor with snaps, also served as a headrest and cushion. Below the first-aid kit are the safety-harness roller and, *to the lower left*, parts of the safety harnesses. The top of the canopy is to the upper right. *National Museum of the United States Air Force*

The bottom of a P-39Q nose is viewed facing forward. The access cover for the reduction gear oil drains is open and hanging from a chain; a vent is in the cover. The nose landing-gear strut has been removed, revealing its mounting bracket and the driveshaft. *National Museum of the United States Air Force*

A blast tube completely encloses the .50-caliber gun barrel protruding from the left gun pod of a P-39Q. On the bottom is a chute for spent cartridge cases. A long ammunition box in the wing fed rounds to the machine gun, which was manually charged before takeoff. *National Museum of the United States Air Force*

A 75-gallon auxiliary fuel tank is shackled to the centerline rack under a P-39Q-15-BE. The tank was manufactured by US Rubber. On the upper front of it is the filler cap. The tubular sway braces of the centerline rack kept the tank from shifting during flight. *National Museum of the United States Air Force*

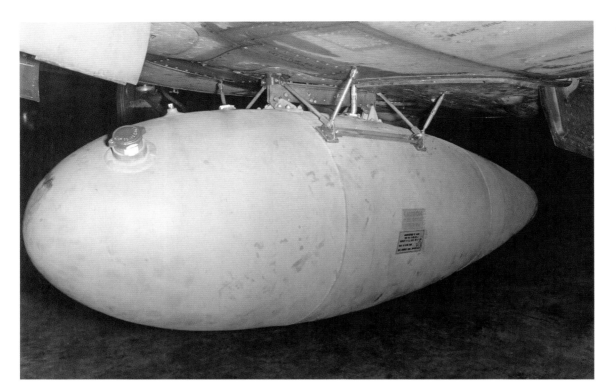

An aluminum 75-gallon auxiliary fuel tank made by Alcoa is viewed from the left front, as installed on a P-39Q-15-BE. The top sticker on the tank cautions that the plug outlet is not in use, while the lower sticker identifies the manufacturer and part number. *National Museum of the United States Air Force*

P-39Q-5-BE, serial number 42-19597, displays a bare-aluminum finish and a ferrying fuel tank below the fuselage. These 175-gallon tanks, used in noncombat ferrying flights, gave the plane a much-greater range than the 75-gallon auxiliary fuel tanks. *American Aviation Historical Society*

Bell P-39Q-20-BE, serial number 44-3572, is viewed from the side. Protruding from the front of the propeller spinner is the sleeve enclosing the 37 mm cannon muzzle. P-39Q-20-BEs transferred to the Soviets reportedly lacked the .50-caliber gun pods. *American Aviation Historical Society*

Flight Officer Willie D. Collins, 363rd Fighter Group, poses next to the left .50-caliber machine gun pod of a P-39Q. The blast tube is not present, and the perforated cooling jacket over the machine gun barrel is visible. A small detail is visible below the gun pod: mounted on crosspieces between the outer sides of the spent-casing ejector are four vertical tines. These probably were designed to guide the spent casings down and away from the pod. The ammunition boxes for the underwing machine guns held 1,000 rounds each. Flight Officer Collins was killed in action on March 4, 1944. *National Museum of the United States Air Force*

Lt. William E. Bullard of the 382nd Fighter Squadron proudly stands by his P-39Q-10-BE, which displays kill symbols for three Japanese aircraft. He is wearing a type A-4 flying suit, winter flying helmet, goggles, and parachute harness. During World War II, Lieutenant Bullard was awarded the Distinguished Flying Cross with six clusters and the Purple Heart. Next to Bullard is a 75-gallon auxiliary fuel tank of a different design than the US Rubber example seen previously. This fuel tank lacks a circumferential seam and was fabricated from aluminum. *National Museum of the United States Air Force*

P-39Qs of the 46th Fighter Squadron, 15th Fighter Group, are parked at an airfield on Makin in the Gilbert Islands in December 1943, within a month after the US capture of that island. The closest plane is P-39Q-1-BE, serial number 42-19499. *National Museum of the United States Air Force*

The propeller spinner of "Little Hinx-Jinx II," a P-39Q of the 82nd Tactical Reconnaissance Squadron in the Southwest Pacific, has been removed, showing the 37 mm cannon muzzle where it exits through the propeller hub. *National Museum of the United States Air Force*

A group of USAAF personnel pose for their photo next to "Mona II," a P-39Q, probably somewhere in the Pacific theater. Risqué pinup art is painted on the gun bay cover. A pointed, tubular muzzle cover has been placed on the end of the blast tube of the pod-mounted .50-caliber machine gun. *San Diego Air & Space Museum*

A flight line of Bell Airacobras, including several P-39Qs in the foreground, include some interesting nicknames on the gun bay covers. The closest plane is marked "Shreveport Sack Rat," followed by "Eileen," "Reba," and "Julia 2nd." Like the nicknames, the pilots' names are written in decorative script, below the windshields. In the far background is "Ruth-Less 2nd," with the nickname written in block letters. *San Diego Air & Space Museum*

A weathered P-39Q-15-BE devoid of markings save for its tail number, 42738, rests at an airfield next to several trainers. A characteristic of the -15 production block was that there were only two oxygen bottles, as opposed to four in earlier production blocks. *American Aviation Historical Society*

P-39Q-10-BE, serial number 42-20879, displays the light-gray exhaust staining on the side of the fuselage aft of the exhausts that was typical for Airacobras. On February 8, 1944, this plane crashed on takeoff at Leesburg Army Air Field, Florida, and was written off. *Stan Piet collection*

A mechanic fills out a report in a faded, begrimed P-39Q Airacobra at Wright Field, near Dayton, Ohio. The silhouette of the right underwing .50-caliber machine gun pod is visible. The national insignia is the type introduced in August 1943. *Stan Piet collection*

Two mechanics service components in the gun bay in a P-39Q. The .50-caliber gun pods have been removed from under the wings, but the two .50-caliber machine guns remain mounted. *Stan Piet collection*

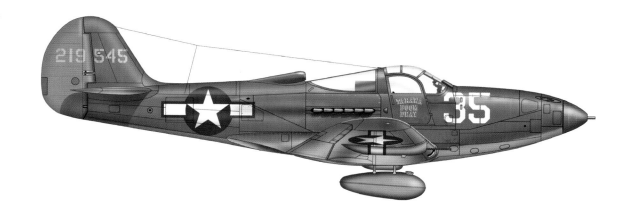

"Tarawa Boom Deay," P-39Q-1-BE, USAAF serial number 42-19544, was assigned to Maj. Joseph H. Powell of the 72nd Fighter Squadron, 21st Fighter Group, in the Marianas Islands in 1944.

P-39s of the 404th Fighter-Bomber Group, based at Myrtle Beach Army Air Field, South Carolina, include the third P-39Q-1-BE produced (*in the foreground*). Its spinner, fuselage band, and tail number were yellow. The other two aircraft are P-39N-1-BEs. *National Archives*

Bell P-39Q-1-BE, serial number 42-19551, nicknamed "Devastating Devil," was painted in a sand over light-blue camouflage from March to December 1943. The plane was assigned to the 46th Fighter Squadron, 15th Fighter Group. Subsequently, the aircraft was repainted in Olive Drab over Neutral Gray camouflage.

A pilot of the 382nd Fighter Squadron prepares to enter the cockpit of a P-39Q-1-BE, serial number 42-19519, while ground crewmen and another pilot stand by on the tarmac. When this squadron went to Europe, it would fly P-51s with the 363rd Fighter Group. *National Museum of the United States Air Force*

Pvt. Charles Hasher, of the 2nd Raider Battalion, stands watch over a P-39Q at the fighter airfield on Cape Torokina, Bougainville, in the Solomon Islands in December 1943. A nickname, part of which appears to be "Vivienne," is written on the fuselage. *National Archives*

P-39Qs taxi down the runway at Cape Torokina prior to taking off on a mission on December 12, 1943. This airfield had been completed just two days earlier, and the runway was constructed of steel matting. Construction equipment is seen in the background. *National Archives*

P-39Q-20-BE, serial number 44-3172, was transferred to the Free French during World War II. This aircraft had the underwing machine-gun pods and a centerline auxiliary fuel tank. On the bottom of the fuselage, directly below the dorsal mast antenna, was a ventral whip antenna.

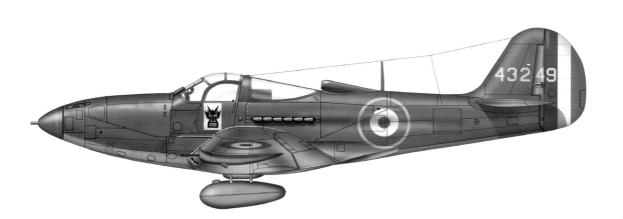

Bell P-39Q-20-BE, serial number 44-3249, was assigned to Groupe de Chasse III/6 of the Forces Aériennes Françaises Libres (Free French Air Forces) in 1944 and operated along the coast of Africa. On the door is the unit's devil's-head insignia.

Airacobras bound for the Soviet air force are parked at Ladd Army Air Field, Fairbanks, Alaska, in July 1943. At least the four closest aircraft with visible tail numbers are P-39Q-5-BEs. Toward the left is a tank trailer, replenishing the planes for the ferry flight. While these Airacobra are being flown across the Bering Sea, most left the US afloat, aboard freighters. *National Museum of the United States Air Force*

Sometimes Airacobras were partially disassembled and packed in crates for shipment overseas, as was the case with this P-39Q-15-BE, which is being lowered onto a pallet. Masking paper protects the surfaces where the wings and empennage have been removed.

US lieutenant Thompson Highfill of the 99th Bomb Group stands in front of a Soviet P-39 flanked by Soviet fliers: one, whose name was recorded as Andrea Hincerockur, and the other, Korzun Venzopkin, in June 1944. The Soviets appreciated the P-39's capabilities and ordered about 5,000 of them, although many were lost during transit to the USSR. *National Museum of the United States Air Force*

Bell P-39Q-15-BE, serial number 44-2547, was piloted by Capt. Grigory Andreyevich Rechkalov of 16th Guards Fighter Aviation Regiment in Ukraine in mid-1944. It was painted Olive Drab over Neutral Gray. Recorded as the second-ranking Allied fighter ace of the war, Rechkalov racked up fifty-six personal kills and five shared kills. The three Cyrillic letters aft of the red star, РГА (RGA), are Rechkalov's initials, which served as his call sign.

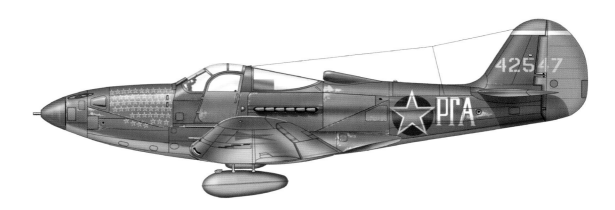

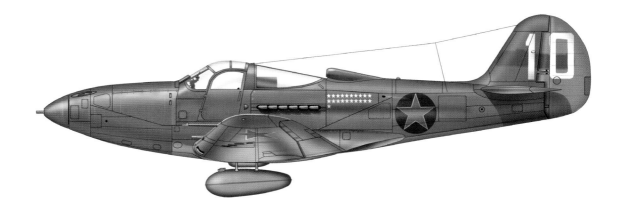

Col. Pavel Stepanovich Kutakhov of 19th Guards Fighter Aviation Regiment of the Soviet air force flew this P-39Q marked with a large, white number 10 on the tail in late 1943. Following the war, Kutakhov served as commander in chief of the Soviet air forces from 1969 to 1984 and was made chief marshal of aviation in 1972. He died in 1984.

A P-39Q-10-BE bearing the aircraft number X72 on the side of the nose stands by on an airfield hardstand. A whip antenna is faintly visible below the fuselage aft of the 75-gallon auxiliary fuel tank. The dorsal mast antenna was not always present on P-39Qs. *Stan Piet collection*

The Commemorative Air Force's P-39Q-5-BE, Bell construction number 21-9597 and Army Air Forces serial number 42-19597, is viewed from various angles during a flight in this sequence of photos. This plane lacks the sleeve over the 37 mm cannon muzzle on the front of the propeller spinner. *Rich Kolasa*

This aircraft is the second P-39Q-5 built. After its stateside service, it was declared surplus, and suffered an engine failure in route to the disposal field, and made an emergency landing in Hobbs, New Mexico. Rather than repair the aircraft, it was transferred to the nearby Capitan High School, who in 1962, sold the aircraft to an individual, show subsequently donated it to the CAF, who eventually returned it to the air in 1974. Since then it has worn a variety of paint schemes. *Rich Kolasa*

The pilot's head is visible through the window of the right cockpit door on the P-39Q. Aft of the cockpit door are the six right exhaust stubs of the Allison V-1710-85 engine. *Rich Kolasa*

The CAF's P-39Q-5-BE is viewed from the lower aft-left quarter. *Rich Kolasa*

The plane is making a landing approach, landing gear and flaps extended, showing the oleo struts at full extension when not bearing the load of the aircraft. Recommended landing speed was between 95 and 100 miles per hour. *Rich Kolasa*

The P-39's pilot manual instructed that when landing, the pilot should "forget that the ship has a tricycle[-]type landing gear and make a normal type landing . . . where the nose of the airplane is well up and the main wheels touch the ground before the nose-wheel (in other words a landing attitude equivalent to that with a conventional gear)." *Rich Kolasa*

The CAF's P-39Q-5-BE taxis after a landing. As seen here, the flaps were to be retracted during taxiing. *Rich Kolasa*

The P-39Q is taxiing with flaps raised, ailerons at the neutral position, and the elevators slightly raised. *Rich Kolasa*

The CAF P-39Q is taxiing with the left aileron slightly depressed and the right aileron slightly elevated. In the background is a bubbletop P-51 Mustang. *Rich Kolasa*

A left-side view of the Confederate Air Force's P-39Q shows the left elevator raised approximately to its limit. The red object to the rear of the canopy is a "remove before flight" tag attached to a cover for the carburetor-air scoop. *Rich Kolasa*

Details of the empennage of the CAF's P-39Q are viewed from the left rear of the rudder. Both elevators are fully raised. The rudder was mounted on two hinges riveted to the vertical beam on the rear of the vertical stabilizer, or vertical fin. That beam, partially visible here, has several lightening holes in it. *Rich Kolasa*

Among the features shown here are the left engine exhaust stubs, the left engine cowling panels, the carburetor air-intake scoop, and the main landing-gear doors. *Rich Kolasa*

As seen in a view of the left main landing gear and its bay, facing to the rear, each main gear was supplied with three doors: one on the inboard side of the gear bay, and two on the oleo strut, which also were called the upper and the lower fairings. These gears were electrically operated and self-locking. *Rich Kolasa*

In a view of the left side of the nose, the round hole in the skin is for inserting a metal tube for use in hoisting the aircraft. A similar hole for the hoist tube is on the opposite side of the nose. Elements of the nose landing gear are evident, including the oleo strut, fork, wheel, antitorque link, and, to the rear of the strut, the radius rod, also referred to as the retracting link. *Rich Kolasa*

Although only faintly visible in this image, on the bottom of each wing is a row of rectangular access doors, each one with a piano hinge on the forward side and three camloc fasteners toward the rear. These doors were for inspecting and adjusting the control-surface cables, wing-attaching bolts, landing gear, and other components. *Rich Kolasa*

The left side of the nose, cockpit, canopy, and engine cowling is displayed. Engine-exhaust smudging is present on the aft part of the cowling and on the fuselage to the rear of the cowling. Details of the wing fillet also are presented. *Rich Kolasa*

The panel marked with the number 68 and the skull and crossbones is the left panel of the gun compartment cowling. This cowling consisted of a top, a left, and a right panel, fastened to the fuselage with camloc fasteners. Visible through the rear section of the canopy is the rollover structure, which protected the pilot in the event of the aircraft flipping over onto the ground. *Rich Kolasa*

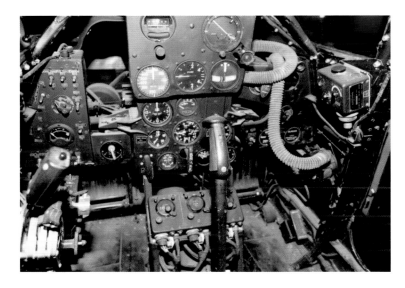

The cockpit of the P-39Q displayed at the National Museum of the United States Air Force features authentic instruments and controls. Toward the right is the pilot's oxygen hose, attached at the bottom to the oxygen regulator. Originally, the rear ends of the two .50-caliber nose machine guns and the gun-charging handles were situated in the openings to the sides of the upper center instrument panel. *National Museum of the United States Air Force*

The power train of a P-39 is displayed. Shown are, *from left to right*, the propeller (with cut-down blades) and spinner, the reduction gearbox, the driveshaft, and the Allison V-1710 engine. The 10-foot-long driveshaft ran at crankcase speed; the reduction gearbox reduced the shaft speed to one that was suitable for driving the propeller. Midway along the driveshaft is the center bearing. Above the driveshaft are the 37 mm cannon and its magazine. *National Museum of the United States Air Force*

The reduction gearbox and propeller are viewed from the right. By having the driveshaft attached to the side of the gearbox, this allowed for the positioning of the 37 mm cannon barrel through the center of the propeller and spinner. *National Museum of the United States Air Force*

The Air Zoo Aerospace and Science Museum, Portage, Michigan, preserves P-39Q-20-BE, USAAF serial number 44-3908. As seen in a frontal view, the plane is painted in RAF-type camouflage of green and tan over gray and has a shark's mouth painted under the nose. *Author*

The aircraft bears camouflage and markings to replicate an Airacobra nicknamed "Whistlin' Britches," which served with the 67th Fighter Squadron on Guadalcanal in 1942. On the left cockpit door is artwork of a rooster wearing boxing gloves. *Author*

The nose landing gear of the Air Zoo's P-39Q is viewed from the right front. When the gear was raised, two side doors and a small, square fairing to the front of the oleo strut served to close the gear bay. *Author*

The nose landing gear is observed from the left side, showing the oleo strut, antitorque link, fork, wheel and tire, antitorque link, and radius rod (or retracting link). Cleveland Pneumatic Tool Co. produced the nose- and main-gear oleo struts for the P-39s. The smooth-contour tire was 19 inches in diameter, and the nosewheel was of a self-castering, nonsteerable design. *Author*

The nosewheel, yoke, and antitorque link are viewed from the rear. The nose-gear fork was of forged steel. Lightening holes were incorporated into the antitorque link. *Author*

The nose landing gear and its bay are viewed from the front of the tire of the nose gear. The front fairing of the bay was bolted to the oleo strut, and that fairing is visible from below. *Author*

The retracting link of the nose landing gear is viewed from the rear, with the gear bay toward the upper right and the bay doors to the sides. The cylinder above the two forks of the retracting link is the retracting screw, which is powered by an electric motor to raise and lower the nose gear. *Author*

The nose landing-gear bay is viewed facing to the rear, showing a bulged panel on the ceiling to provide clearance for the wheel when retracted. Also in view are the rear bulkhead, the plumbing, and the two rear hinges of the side doors of the bay. *Author*

The right side of the cockpit and the engine cowling of the Air Zoo's P-39Q, rebranded "*Whistlin' Britches*," is displayed, showing the twelve right engine exhaust stubs close-up. The rollover structure, with several lightening holes in it, is visible through the aft section of the cockpit canopy. *Author*

The carburetor air-intake scoop is visible to the rear of the right side of the canopy. The scoop and the rear section of the canopy were on aluminum-alloy-sheet panels that were part of the engine cowling, which consisted of eight panels in total. A horizontal splitter was inside the scoop. *Author*

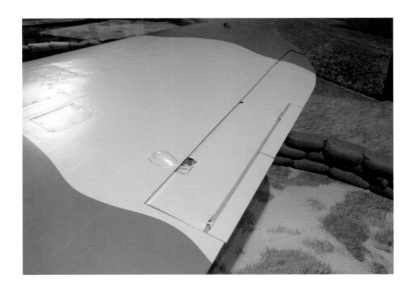

In a view of the top of the right wing, the aileron, with its trim tab (*left*) and servo tab (*right*), are in view. A small, bulged fairing is attached with screws to the wing to the immediate front of the aileron. *Author*

The left side of the empennage of the Air Zoo's P-39Q is displayed. Above the "0" in the number "20" is a small, teardrop-shaped navigation light with a white lens. A similar light is on the right side of the vertical stabilizer. Sometimes, these lights had amber rather than white lenses. *Author*

The P-39Q marked "Whistlin' Britches" is equipped with two imitation machine-gun barrels in each wing, which are not appropriate for that model of Airacobra. On the underside of the wingtip is a green navigation light. A similar light is on the top of the wingtip. Red navigation lights are on the top and the bottom of the left wingtip. *Author*

"Whistlin' Britches" exhibits the sleek contours and streamlined fuselage that were characteristic of the P-39. The fairings, or doors, of the right main landing gear are in view. *Author*

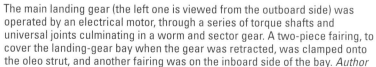

The main landing gear (the left one is viewed from the outboard side) was operated by an electrical motor, through a series of torque shafts and universal joints culminating in a worm and sector gear. A two-piece fairing, to cover the landing-gear bay when the gear was retracted, was clamped onto the oleo strut, and another fairing was on the inboard side of the bay. *Author*

The main landing-gear wheels were of magnesium alloy, and were based on Goodyear drawing number 50094. The hydraulic disc brakes were Goodyear drawing 510548. The tires were size 26-6, made of six-ply rayon, with a high-pressure, puncture-proof inner tubes. *Author*

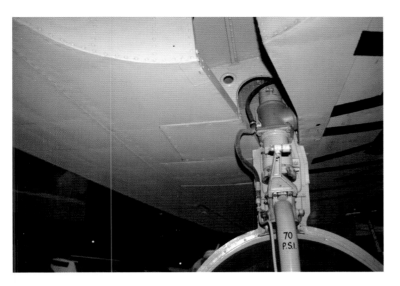

The left main landing gear is observed from the inboard side, showing, *from bottom to top*, the fork, with the recommended tire pressure painted on it; the piston and the antitorque link; the oleo strut; and the spindle assembly, by means of which the strut pivoted when retracted or lowered. *Author*

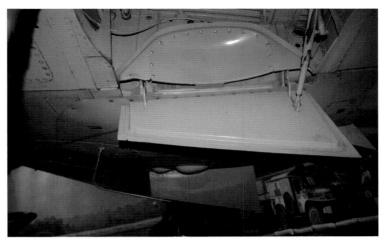

The inboard fairing of the left main landing gear, called the "flipper door" in the P-39 Erection and Maintenance Instructions, is shown in the lowered position. Attached to it is a spring-loaded arm, which acted, in unison with the landing-gear wheel, to push the flipper door open during the lowering of the gear. When the gear was raised, the wheel struck a tab attached to the rod, which caused the flipper door to close. *Author*

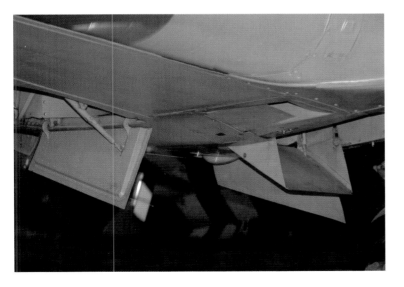

As seen from the rear of the left landing-gear bay, to the left is the flipper door and its spring-loaded actuating and retracting arm. To the right is the open shutter for the engine-coolant radiator air outlet, beyond which is the right flipper door. The oil-cooler shutters are in the closed positions to the sides of the radiator shutter. *Author*

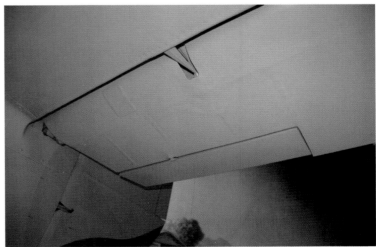

The left horizontal stabilizer and elevator are observed from below. A trim tab is present on the left elevator only. On the elevator between the fuselage and the hinge is a rectangular access panel, fastened with four screws. *Author*

Although many USAAF pilots trained in standard P-39s, a two-seat trainer designated the TP-39 was developed from P-39 airframes. The first such conversion seems to have been from a P-39F. The guns were removed, and a cockpit for the instructor was installed in the former gun bay. A canopy over the new cockpit connected to the canopy over the trainee's cockpit. The instructor's canopy was hinged on the side, while the trainee's cockpit retained the side doors. For better stability, a new dorsal fillet was installed, extending from the rear of the carburetor intake to the vertical fin. A long, low fin was also added to the bottom rear of the fuselage. Two-seat trainers designated the TP-39Q were also converted from P-39Qs, an example of which is shown here. For security reasons, this photo was retouched, with the tail number, 220024, covered over and part of the background painted in. *National Archives*

This insignia, presumably created by Bell Aircraft, was applied to the right side of the fuselage between the cockpits, as seen in the preceding photograph of a TP-39Q. The airman emerging from the tipi has "Plane Pete" written on his overalls. *American Aviation Historical Society*

The tail number is not visible on this TP-39Q, but the nose landing gear has the late-type wheel and tire found on midseries and later P-39s. The outline of the gun-bay access cover remains visible. The exhausts are the six-stub type. *American Aviation Historical Society*

Most of the markings, including the national insignia and tail number, have faded off or have become otherwise obscured on this TP-39. The faint outline of the first two digits of the tail number, 22, are visible. An insignia and the aircraft number, V-99, are visible. *American Aviation Historical Society*

This Bell TP-39Q at a weed-choked hardstand at an airfield, possibly after the end of World War II, was converted from P-39Q-20-BE, serial number 44-3897. The national insignia has been painted over, but the tail number can still be seen. *American Aviation Historical Society*

The pilot of "Connie," the Central Texas Wing of the Commemorative Air Force's P-39Q-5-BE, serial number 42-19597, waves from the cockpit. Today, few P-39s survive, and flying examples are truly rare. This aircraft is painted in glossy Olive Drab over Neutral Gray. The landing-gear struts are painted glossy Olive Drab, or a similar color. *Rich Kolasa*